PYTHON FOR ACCOUNTING & BUSINESS

Volume 1

SHIVAM ARORA, CPA

Shivam Arora

ISBN

978-1-958400-28-9

DEDICATION

To my fellow rower, paddling through the stream of life with my idiosyncrasies and my whims.

TABLE OF CONTENTS

PREFACE

Technology has influenced how business is conducted since the start of the 20th century. Organizations have always rushed to adopt the latest and greatest, and human resource has had to keep pace with this trend. Professionals must keep themselves updated and be ready for quick changes in status quo. Institutes of higher education must keep their curricula updated to match the dynamic nature of today's business.

There was the computer, then there was the internet, and then there were spreadsheets. Now, there is the ability to store massive amounts of data. This has opened new avenues for organizations to make decisions driven by the quantifiable, hard truth of data. Data science has become ubiquitous. Organizations realize its inevitability and have been increasingly developing infrastructure to facilitate data-driven decisions.

Since my undergraduate program, I have continually conducted research in accounting and business using data analytics tools. I realized that accounting, like any other business domain, is awash with data. This data can yield powerful insights when analyzed appropriately. However, many accounting students do not place enough emphasis, in my opinion, on developing data science skills that can set them apart when marketing themselves to an employer.

My goal with this book is to introduce Python, a business-friendly programming language, to accounting and business professionals so that they can prepare for the inevitable data science/machine learning work that is going to be a part of their jobs soon. A secondary goal is to encourage analytical, data-driven approaches to solve problems. Through this book, I also provide a history of the accounting profession and how it has already and is expected to further be molded by fast-paced advancements in technology. Finally, I challenge the general notion that programming languages and advanced analytical techniques are application solely to the IT profession. The power of these technologies is currently being harnessed beautifully in front-end and business-specific domains. While professionals currently develop these through on-the-job experience and hands-on training, my hope with this book is to provide a preliminary background so that professionals may preempt any technology-based surprises as they start their business careers or switch jobs.

This book is the first of a two-volume series that is largely based on my experience as a consultant specializing in the application of data science to accounting and business. While this volume introduces the basics of Python along with select third-party libraries, the next volume delves into more advanced topics to tackle challenging problems faced by today's business professionals. As a CPA, I naturally have more experience in accounting-related tasks. However, this book should be useful to any business professional who has a need for analysis, data science, and/or automation. Something to note: the first few chapters contain background information that I find interesting, but others may not. If you want to directly talk shop, start with Chapter 4.

I am always open to feedback, new ideas, and suggestions. Reach out with your thoughts on the book, suggestions on revisions I should incorporate, new use-cases I should include, and anything else that's relevant. You can connect with me through my LinkedIn account: www.linkedin.com/in/shivam-arorauta

SECTION 01
BACKGROUND

CHAPTER 01 | ACCOUNTING: PAST & PRESENT

Commerce began with the advent of society. People began collecting and storing food, hides, early tools, and other items necessary for their survival. Much like the neighbors of today, they often lent these items or bartered for other goods with their peers. So began the first-known practice of record-keeping: markings on trees, cave walls, and stones to keep track of the fruits they collected, the animals hunted, and the resources shared. These early records signal the birth of accounting.

Records discovered in the remains of well-established cities of the past allow us to understand and trace back the history of the development of accounting practices. We now know how the early bookkeepers, making best use of the knowledge and tools available to them, kept meticulous records of trade and commerce in their age.

THE PAST

EARLY DEVELOPMENTS

As people began to flock together, the first agricultural lands and practices began to develop. They settled down into settlements and towns. Soon thereafter, people were producing goods and resources in surplus which led to the eventual establishment of trade and commerce. In due time, institutions were developed. Governments began to take shape and control, religion organized itself, and merchants sought other settlements to exchange goods. Taxation and trade led to the origination of money and numbers, which then demanded that records be kept – early records of accounts detailing the goods traded, expenditures incurred, and income earned.

In Mesopotamia, accounting records have been found dating back over 7,000 years. These accounts provide tremendous insight into the commerce and economy of the ancient city, shedding light on how early practices of accounting emerged in conjunction with developments in money, counting, writing, and a defined numerical system. Similar records have been found in the remains of Babylon, Sumer, and Assyria.[1][2]

Over the next few centuries, the use of clay tokens and graphical representations of accounts, such as those found in ancient Persia, signaled a significant advancement in the practices of accounting. The emergence of the phonetic alphabet in Phoenicia allowed accountants to improve their bookkeeping practices. Egyptians and Babylonians began conducting financial inspections and tracking goods in the warehouses, creating the first auditing system.[3][4]

The most significant development was then seen in ancient Rome. A few centuries passed by, and a world power emerged: the Roman Empire. Comprehensive documents were found which serve as evidence of how accounting had progressed to include complex and elaborate records of the empire's financial dealings. These scrupulous records of construction, management of the vast military, taxes and public expenditure, decades-long public projects are testimony to the critical role of accountancy in the rise of power of the Roman civilization.[5]

DOUBLE-ENTRY BOOKKEEPING EMERGES

At the beginning of the 9th century, a Persian scholar named Muhammad ibn Musa al-Khwarizmi wrote *al-Kitab al-Mukhtasar fi al-Hisab al-Jabr wal-Muqabalah* (The Compendious Book on Calculation by Completion and Balancing) to resolve the issue of Islamic inheritance which required the use of ratios and mathematical computations based on Hindo-Arabic numerals. The book proved mathematical concepts of algebra (a term derived from al-Khwarizmi, known in Europe as Algorithmi) with the last chapter dedicated to the double-entry bookkeeping system as a means to calculate inheritances.[6]

Al-Khwarizmi's book eventually made its way, through trade and scholarly discourse, to European academic centers and banks. They began to use Hindo-Arabic numerals in their accounting records. Three key algebraic and accounting concepts emerged:

1. 'Debits' should equal 'Credits' (D = C) – algebraic calculations on both sides of an '=' sign must balance each other.
2. Real accounts – a record of a business owner's nominal wealth (assets) less claims against that wealth (liabilities) return the owner's net wealth (equity).
3. Nominal accounts – a record of a business owner's net income through calculations of activities that affect their wealth.

However, one of the most notable developments came from the works of an Italian mathematician and friar, Fra Luca Bartolomeo de Pacioli (or commonly known as simply Luca Pacioli). His treatise, *Summa de arithmetica, geometria, proportioni et proportionalita* (Summary of arithmetic, geometry, proportions, and proportionality), published in 1494, is an extensive textbook on mathematics and accounting. The book contains the first printed documentation on the double-entry bookkeeping system and explained the advantages of using Hindo-Arabic numerals in accounting and mathematics.[2][7]

He included a chapter titled *Particularis de computis et scripturis* ("Details of calculation and recording") describing various accounting methods. He explained the double-entry bookkeeping, trial balances, balance sheets, and many other accounting tools still in use by professional accountants today. He also explained the *Rule of 72*, which is used for predicting the future value of an investment. Pacioli's guidance and instructions on bookkeeping were so monumental in improving accounting and auditing practices that he is now known as the 'Father of Accounting and Bookkeeping' in Europe. He was the first person to publish and describe in detail the double-entry system, allowing others to study and employ its use in their businesses.[2][7]

Double-entry bookkeeping presented several significant advantages over the traditional uncoordinated ways employed by accountants in the past. The most substantial being:

1. It accentuated the dual nature of business transactions – all debit entries must have corresponding credit entries.
2. It became proof of accurate accounting as total debit must equal total credit.

3. It allowed accountants to produce statements of income, equity, assets, and liabilities through the integration of personal, real, and nominal accounts.
4. It allowed for comprehensive and orderly recording of the financial aspects of business transactions.

Double-entry bookkeeping system was so successful that it helped merchants and banks scale their businesses across cities, grow, and even prevent losses at times of major crises.[8]

THE PRESENT

THE FIRST STEPS TOWARD MODERN ACCOUNTING

Around 1600, joint-stock companies began to emerge. Investments from multiple sources required a comprehensive presentation of financial records to garner the interest of investors. However, different accounting techniques were felt necessary to analyze information internally. Two accounting systems were subsequently developed: *management accounting* (internal) and *financial accounting* (external). In addition, the demand for independent audits of external accounts grew for the purposes of attestation. Even then, up until the 1800s, investments were frequently made without knowledge of financials, and as such, involved a risk that made investing attractive only to the wealthy.[9][10]

The Industrial Revolution, from 1760-1820 and 1840, led to mass production and manufacturing, and increased competition for profits. As businesses grew, so did the demand for professional bookkeepers to create and manage complex financial documents and records. Huge capital movements, widespread construction of factories, management of thousands of employees, and the manufacturing and distribution of goods at large scale demanded even more extensive financial planning, statements, and records.[11][12]

Around the same time, railroads had been set up allowing for greater movement of goods and people. The development of railroads, especially in the United States, was a major milestone in the progress of accounting. Accountants were needed to provide cost estimates, create financial statements, calculate operating ratios, generate production reports, and produce a plethora of other financial documents for trade and commerce.[2]

In addition to these advancements, the development of large corporations and the scale of their operations meant that accountants had to develop novel methods of completing their tasks. As such, formalized accounting organizations began to emerge around the world.[2]

ACCOUNTING BECOMES A PROFESSION

In the early 19th century, the first professionalization of accountants took place as the profession of chartered accountants came into being in Scotland. In 1854, a petition was presented to Queen Victoria by the Institute of Accountants for a royal charter. The members of the institute insisted that accountants have existed for a long time in Scotland and that the accountants required knowledge of the law as consultants to courts on financial matters. After the royal charter was granted, the members were dubbed 'Chartered Accountants.'[12]

Soon thereafter, pressed by the demands of the Industrial Revolution in Britain, large-scale manufacturing, and an increase in global trade, the Institute of Chartered Accountants in England and Wales was set up in 1880.[12]

In the United States, the *American Association of Public Accountants* (now known as the American Institute of Certified Public Accountants [AICPA]) was set up in 1887 to tackle similar issues. The formal recognition of the profession came in 1896 when the role of *Certified Public Accountant* (CPA) was established.[2]

CPAs today must go through rigorous educational, experience, and ethical requirements to acquire and maintain licensure. While licensing requirements vary by state, standard minimum requirements include possessing a baccalaureate degree, completing at least 150-semester units of college education, successfully passing the Uniform CPA Exam set by AICPA, and acquiring at least one year of "non-routine" accounting work experience.[13]

The CPA exam includes auditing and attestation (AUD), regulation (REG), financial accounting and reporting (FAR), and business environment and concepts (BEC). Most states also require aspirants to complete some form of exam on ethics.[13]

Once a CPA license has been obtained, holders are required to participate in and complete continuing professional education (CPE) to renew their license. Again, state requirements vary, but an average of 40 hours of CPE is standard. Some states require CPAs to take an ethics course every alternate license renewal.[13]

TECHNOLOGICAL DISRUPTIONS IN ACCOUNTANCY

Developments in technology have significantly altered the landscape of accounting. William Seward Burroughs' invention of the adding machine in 1887 and its subsequent versions for commercial use was monumental in aiding accountants' calculation of receipts and related bookkeeping.[14]

Then, in 1946, the creation of credit cards marked the first notable step toward digital financial transactions. IBM's release of their large computers in 1952 was the next major step in the digital journey that accountants were soon to embark upon. The computer was easy for businesses to install in their companies and accountants were the first people to employ its use. Over the decades, computers became smaller and portable allowing for greater access and more advanced tools for accountants to speed up their processes, improve the accuracy of their data, and produce complex reports in a short time.[2]

The development of Enterprise Resource Planning (ERP) software made it easier for accountants to track business resources and commitments. Eventually, the introduction of SaaS computing and cloud technology enabled greater automation, integration, and scalability across various platforms used for accounting.[15]

However, the most pressing disruptions have occurred since the early 2010s. Advancements in machine learning (ML) and artificial intelligence (AI) have helped businesses leverage the exponential benefits of these progressive technologies. Today, several firms make use of AI and ML to establish financial policies, analyze audit reports, and identify patterns for improvements. Automated data-entry systems and robots for personal financial advice are in practice today.[15]

The availability of tools such as MS Office Suite, QuickBooks, Sage, Xero, IDEA, etc., have allowed for previously unimaginable ease, speed, and accuracy in accounting. The ever-increasing complexity of accounting, combined with the development of programming languages, blockchain, and quantum technology will pave the way into the future. However, for the majority chunk of practitioners, concerns still abound.

THE NEXT STEPS

Increased dependability on technology has caused global concerns amongst accountants, auditors, and business professionals worldwide that their jobs will become redundant, taken over by mass automation and artificial intelligence. The reliance of present-day accountants on these tools to deliver financial reports and accounting documents has become worrisome. However, according to a 2020 study by Sora Yoon [Ajou University, Korea], global economic situation since 2015 and the COVID-19 pandemic has shown that that is far from the truth. Businesses that faced crises were able to navigate their way out using intelligent financial planning and creative (legal) strategizing guided by CPAs. Developments in cloud technology, blockchain, artificial intelligence, and machine learning have helped businesses and accountants adapt to the changing global work environment and tactfully deal with challenges presented during the pandemic. Accountants, therefore, do not have to fear AI taking over their jobs – they need to concern themselves with adapting to and embracing emerging technology.[16][17]

Accountants must understand that modern tools and AI can optimize their roles by doing the "grunt work." They can take care of manual, repetitive, and time-consuming processes, allowing accountants to focus on the strategic and creative aspects of their work.[17]

Today's accountant should be able to form a symbiotic relationship with emerging technologies. Automation can span across the broad spectrum of audits, payroll management, taxation, and banking. Modern technology can help:

1. Download multiple files from the internet, including AR/AP invoices.
2. Transform scanned/handwritten PDFs into digital text using optical character recognition (OCR).
3. Employ machine learning to automatically complete journal entries and ledger postings.
4. Automatically fill in PDF forms.
5. Routinely calculate wages, deductions, pensions, dispensation, and allow for access to pay slips.

6. Generate analysis reports on business profitability, cash flow, growth, and other performance indicators.
7. Reduce clutter through deduplication of records and files, leading to faster retrieval of information.

Professionals who adapt to new technologies will be able to strengthen businesses and companies through financial planning, refined budgets, compliance, and become indispensable members of the strategic and creative units of their companies. These technologies will allow accountants to take on complex, challenging, and ever-changing problems faced by the businesses of tomorrow, even more so than they do today. Learning a programming language can set accountants and business professionals apart.

CHAPTER 02 | **AN INTRODUCTION: PYTHON & BUSINESS**

Over the recent past, data production has been spurred on by technological advancements. According to International Data Corporation's (IDC) *The Digitization of the World: From Edge to Core*, annual compounded growth rate of data is about 61%. The total world data is expected to reach an enormous 175 zettabytes [175,000,000,000,000 gigabytes] by 2025.[18]

A lot of this data falls within the business domain. To cope with this massive surge, business professionals need to learn to code and understand artificial intelligence and machine learning.

WHAT IS PYTHON?

Developed in 1991 by Guido van Rossum, Python is an interpreted, object-oriented, high-level, multipurpose programming language. Its dynamic semantics have roots in the English language, which make it one of the easiest languages to learn. Python has grown in popularity because it is freely available, open-source, and boasts a massive collection of libraries which is continually supported and updated by a worldwide community.[19]

At its core, Python is designed to be straightforward. Its minimalist nature emphasizes readability, fluency, and simplicity. Its language constructs and object orientation are designed to allow programmers to easily write clear and logical code for projects of all sizes.[20]

The developers of Python wanted it to be an easy and fun language. Even the name is derived from the British comedy group, Monty Python, who are often referenced in the language's tutorials. Avid users of the programming language are popularly called *Pythonistas*.[21]

WHY PYTHON?

Python is a versatile language that can be used to create small, automated tasks, such as a support bot for an internal website, or highly complex and large-scale projects, including analyzing huge quantities of data for an investment company.[22]

Its scalability across businesses of all sizes, implementation of machine learning algorithms, and data mining capabilities make it an appealing programming language, especially for CPAs and the broader financial industry.[23]

Python offers several advantages as a programming language:

Easy To Read

Python's code looks much like free-flowing English and is easily understandable by users who are not "core" programmers. This makes it attractive to those who've just begun to code and/or are learning mainly for assistance with daily work (as opposed to core software development).[24]

High-Level/General-Purpose Programming

Python has easy-to-read structures which are interpreted off a low-level language (the one used by your computer's processor). Using an interpreter allows for Python's seamless portability without the need for alterations. It is also a general-purpose language with applications across a wide array of fields, enabling developers and end-users alike to take advantage.[25]

Object-Orientated Programming

Python is object-oriented. Object-oriented programming (OOP) allows for replicability and the creation of systemic components by structuring bundles of related properties and functions into individual, distinct objects. This helps to create a clear program structure and easily maintain, modify, and reuse code.[26]

Development Speed

As a dynamic programming language, Python is concise and productive because it doesn't require you to build applications from scratch but allows you to use different components together. The vast library-base and readily available support help accelerate development.[23]

Flexibility/Versatility

Python allows users to choose between object-oriented and procedural programming. It can be used across different types of projects. Additionally, it allows flexibility regarding data types and sizes.[23]

Portability

Since Python is a high-level programming language, it relies on an interpreter. This reliance enables identical interpretation of a script across various operating systems, including Windows, Mac OS, Linux, and UNIX, with little to no need for modifications. It also allows developers to implement portable graphical user interfaces (GUI).[23]

Powerful Libraries

Perhaps the biggest advantage that Python offers is its collection of readily available third-party libraries. A library can be thought of as a group of pre-written codes available to use in your projects. The Python Standard Library includes syntaxes, tokens, and modules, whereas the Python Package Index (PyPI) is a repository of software and components for writing programs, testing, web browser scripting, database management, graphics, email servers, and more.[23][26]

ACCOUNTING WORK USING PYTHON

There are several accounting tasks that can be automated using Python. From basic data entry to advanced cash flow reporting, CPAs can leverage Python to improve speed, accuracy, and efficiency. For the purposes of understanding, I have grouped these as intermediate and advanced tasks.

INTERMEDIATE

Data Entry

Accountants often spend hours manually entering data and information from physical and electronic documents; this time can be greatly reduced using OCR-based scanning tools which can capture and feed data directly into accounting software which can be synced to different tools almost instantaneously. It is possible to integrate OCR systems and engines, such as OCRopus and Tesseract, into Python programming to read, identify, store, and collate data.[27]

Invoice Processing

Invoicing programs automatically generate electronic invoices (with the added benefit of saving stationery costs), keep track of invoices that have been paid, and issue reminders for those that are overdue. Invoicing recognition software also enables accurate capture of relevant data from print invoices, reducing errors resulting from manual data entry. Automation and cloud technology in sync enable accountants to store invoices in a safe, secure place for quick retrieval of invoices when needed.[27]

Python can be used to create an API to retrieve invoices from emails, read and extract data from each document, and validate it based on set business rules. Once done, the program can generate a final report which contains the complete invoice data for a set period, and then export it as a file or store it within the ERP system.[27]

Expense Reporting

Python can help categorize expenses, generate real-time expense reports, save time on manually rummaging through receipts, and even save companies money spent on reimbursing employees from over-stated expenses.[28]

Monthly Reporting

Monthly reporting involves many laborious tasks that can be automated to save time and improve efficiency. These can include rectification of errors, data transfer between different programs, receipts and payments reconciliation, and deduplication. Automating these tasks and quick data processing can help generate monthly financial reports. Python programming can allow CPAs to extract data from a database, process it into a format of choice, and present it as a concise report using data visualization libraries.[28]

Payroll Management

Automated payroll management programs can calculate wages, taxes, deductions, and pensions. Companies can transfer pay directly to employee accounts via automated electronic banking and employees can securely access their pay slips online. Python programming can be used to develop GUI-based desktop and web payroll management systems for the calculation, distribution, and reporting of employee salaries efficiently, quickly, and accurately.[26]

Customer Support Service

It is important for professionals to maintain a seamless communication channel and record with their clients. A customer relationship management (CRM) program helps in scheduling automated reminders, keep track of conversation in single threads, maintain notes, provide ease of access to shared documents, and improve overall communication. Python is an ideal programming language for developing CRMs since they comprise of several different components working together. It offers efficient metaprogramming by allowing code inspection and modification in real-time. Additionally, Python is useful for both core implementation and scripting of the program, easing its complexity and improving the overall flexibility.[29]

Payments Management

Automation helps in promptly receiving due payments from clients or making payments to vendors. Online programs help with the collection of recurring debt payments, reduce time spent on debt collection, and improve cash flow practices. For instance, Python can be used on e-commerce platforms for complete accounting, inventory management, fraud monitoring, and payments disbursement using an API on the website or mobile application.[26]

Document Collaboration

Cloud storage and data integration tools ported through Python allow professionals to store and retrieve client information and files safely, securely, and efficiently. These files can then be shared or referred to quickly with clients. Document collaboration also enables accountants to connect files with other tools for automated data processing, data entry, data analysis, and report generation.[28]

ADVANCED

Big Data Handling

Rapid increases in data volumes in need of processing require automation to be completed without human error using bots. Automation significantly improves output speed, accuracy, and reliability. Python allows for automation of millions of data entries which can be processed and analyzed in a fraction of a time compared to manual processing. Auditors working with smaller sample sizes can work with the entire data population (this is possible but perhaps very debatable!). Taxes on thousands of transactions can be automatically calculated, filed, and even paid using the proper tools.[30]

Cash Flow Forecasting

CPAs serve as advisors and provide valuable financial insights to help with strategic business decisions. They must be able to gather data with accuracy and present it in a compelling, clear, and concise way. Automated workflows using Python, often in conjunction with other tools, allow them to create pipelines for data processing while also identifying data challenges. Clean data is a prerequisite to accurate cash flow forecasting, which can be performed using sophisticated machine learning models in Python.[31]

Advanced Automating

Advanced automating is extremely useful in processing bulk tasks, such as downloading thousands of files, scanning them using OCR, neatly compiling the information in an Excel sheet and linking it to corresponding files in cloud storage. Python allows accountants to create a batch of instructions based on keyboard and mouse strokes to program multiple steps of a task into a quick shortcut.[32]

Machine Learning

Machine learning allows for greater automation of tasks where large amounts of data need to be processed and analyzed. The use of classes and objects in Python-based programs allows for integration of ML where tasks do not follow a strict format. For example, ML can help with such things as predict lease classification as *operating* or *finance* by 'learning' from lease contracts.[33]

DEBUNKING MYTHS AROUND PROGRAMMING

Programming is expensive and challenging to learn

Accounting firms often acquire custom-built software to automate tasks. These programs are expensive and often fail to produce the desired results. However, modern developments in software development have made it relatively straightforward for anyone to learn coding and develop software, tools, and applications based on their own research and goals.

Python is open-source, with many free or low-cost tutorials and courses available online. It is easy to understand, learn, and use due to the readability of its code and accessibility to its vast collection of libraries. Compared to other languages, Python also has a smaller learning curve and is more "business-oriented."

Automation will only save labor-costs

While automation saves labor costs, it also has other benefits. Automating business tasks directly improves accuracy, speed, and reliability of output. [37]

It is particularly important for accounting firms dealing with large quantities of data that are in the process of expansion. More clients mean more data. Although automation certainly saves labor costs as bots continue to work ceaselessly on data analysis and processing, other benefits including better accuracy and reliability in data processing, and a general improvement in employees' technical skill level must also be noted.

Programming is a concept of the future

Programming and automation have been around for some time. There have, however been significant advances over the past couple of decades, and we are now moving into an age where they are no longer a choice but are rapidly becoming a necessity.

Automation gives people more control over their work. By selectively choosing which aspects of your work you want bots to process, you can optimize your work.

Only large corporations can automate

It might have been true once that only large companies can automate due to high-costs and resources required; however, modern tools and programming languages have widened reach.

Smaller firms can automate tasks with readily available and inexpensive tools. Python has made it easy for accountants to learn how to code and automate tasks without relying on third-party vendors or purchasing expensive programs. Automation today, with the resources available, is for everyone. [40]

WHY PREFER PYTHON OVER OTHER LANGUAGES?

Because I am biased towards it! But seriously, I think none of the other languages boasts all the advantages of Python discussed above. Every other language falls short in at least one aspect. Some are not object-oriented, making it difficult to logically group code. Others are low-level and, although faster, are not easily understandable. Yet others are not as widely supported.

Perhaps the biggest reason I am such a strong proponent of Python is its massive library-base. There is a library available in Python for virtually everything. There are libraries for core programming work such as web development, and there are also libraries for business-specific work such as scanning invoices and filling PDF forms. Python also boasts one of the largest selections of machine learning/forecasting libraries. Interestingly enough, there is also a library to randomly generate jokes.

While professionals can choose to learn any of the other languages that would help them with their work, I prefer Python for the many advantages, as discussed above, it has to offer compared to others.

CHAPTER 03 | **WHY SHOULD YOU CARE?**

The corporate world is evolving at an unprecedented pace. Modern businesses are facing novel challenges and must adapt new practices if they are to thrive in the business environment of the future. Over the next few decades, significant economic changes will further influence decisions the leaders of tomorrow must take.[35][41]

Surge in population (expected to reach 9.8 billion people by 2050), longer human lifespans, and demographic changes with more women and a younger workforce will impact career opportunities worldwide. In addition, modern employees' preferences for multinational work prospects, workplace flexibility, teamwork, and organizational culture are already influencing how employers hire people and develop their teams.[36][42]

The predicted shift in economic power from Western countries, primarily six of the G7 nations (USA, UK, Japan, Canada, France, Germany, Italy) to the Eastern E7 (Turkey, China, Brazil, Indonesia, India, Russia, Mexico) is likely to increase employment opportunities in these countries with a diverse talent pool.[37]

Technological disruptions stimulate continual change in global commerce. There is a high demand for data analytics which is synchronous with advancements in computing technology, adaption of artificial intelligence, developments in cloud solutions, and a massive increase in global data output.[38][43]

In this context, progressive leaders of today rely on CPAs and business professionals to analyze big data for better decision making to gain advantage over competition. [39][44]

IMPORTANCE OF MODERN CPAs

Professional accountants are at the forefront of quality financial reporting, decision making, and efforts to protect public interest. Businesses rely on accountants to develop corporate strategy, help with cost management, and mitigate risks.[40]

Accountants wear many hats. Their responsibilities vary depending on the role they perform within an organization. CPAs, on the board of directors, help govern companies. When performing internal audits, they provide assurance regarding the organization's financial reporting, governance, internal controls, and risk management along with recommendations on areas of improvement. As chief financial officers (CFOs), they supervise financial health through strategic management of financial information. In academia, they impart knowledge to the professionals of tomorrow.[45]

Arguably the most integral role of a CPA is within the public sector. Public accountants provide accounting, auditing, taxation, advisory, and consulting services to other organizations. As watchdogs of integrity, drivers of fiscal policies, and authorities on ethics, accountants affect the economy and influence public lives at large.[45]

Safeguarding Public Trust

Professional accountants bear the responsibility of maintaining public trust in the financial system by assisting organizations with accurate financial reporting and ethical operations. Public trust and value are borne out of confidence the public has in the authenticity of financial data produced by a business. There are established accounting standards to promote standardization, and auditors support public trust by assuring that financial statements follow these standards.

However, CPAs often face the dilemma of meeting their organizational demands over protecting public interest. At times, accountants may be asked to modify certain information in financial records to meet financial targets. It is here that the emphasis laid by accounting regulatory bodies on ethics comes into play. CPAs are held to high standards and must perform their roles with integrity and objectivity to maintain public trust and, as a result, interest in the financial system.[46]

Accountants have always enjoyed respect in society. During the COVID-19 pandemic, this role was further amplified because businesses, public, and even entire economies relied on CPAs to guide them through chaos and disruption.[48]

Certification – A Mark of Competence and Ethics

Obtaining the CPA certification is a multistep process. State requirements vary, but CPAs in general must obtain a bachelor's degree, complete 150-hours of education with mandatory accounting/business courses, pass the Uniform CPA Exam, and gain at least a year of qualified work experience. These exacting requirements ensure that accounting professionals can competently, professionally, and truthfully provide services.[47][48]

Professional accountants are required to comply with the following fundamentals:

1. **Integrity**
   To be straightforward and honest in all professional relationships.

2. **Objectivity**
   To not allow bias, conflict of interest or undue influence of others to override professional or business judgments.

3. **Professional Competence and Due Care**
   To maintain professional knowledge and skill at a level required to ensure that a client or employer receives competent professional services based on current developments in practice, legislation and techniques, and act diligently and in accordance with applicable technical and professional standards.

4. **Confidentiality**
   To respect the confidentiality of information acquired because of professional and business relationships and not disclose any such information to third parties without proper and specific authority, unless there is a legal or professional duty to disclose.

5. **Professional Behavior**
   To comply with relevant laws and regulations and avoid any action that discredits the profession.

SKILL GAPS

Accountants are integral. However, massive amounts of data, technological disruptions, increased regulations, rigorous compliance, and, recently, the remote work culture propagated by COVID-19 has put more demands on the profession. These changes have created a skill gap between the professional accountants of today and what they are expected to achieve tomorrow.

The National Association of State Boards of Accountancy (NASBA) and the American Institute of Certified Public Accountants (AICPA) conducted a survey of top accounting firms. They discovered that there is a considerable skill gap resulting from current accounting educational programs. Employers emphasized that accountants need to have better knowledge and skills related to data analytics, IT audit, systems, and cybersecurity.[51]

New CPA graduates are expected to be familiar with the latest technology and develop skills in programming.[50] Repetitive work previously handled by accountants is increasingly being shifted to AI/ML; experienced accountants are now expected to take positions of critical thinkers and problem solvers.

There are two significant domains where accountants are required to gain deeper knowledge and build better skills.

Technology

Employers now look for professional accountants who can demonstrate technical skills in the following areas:[59]

1. Programming languages such as Python
2. Legacy technologies such as Microsoft Excel or Access
3. Structured and unstructured databases
4. Data analysis tools
5. Data visualization tools
6. Exploratory data analysis
7. Documenting analysis
8. Statistical analysis
9. Machine learning and predictive tools

10. Text mining and HTML scraping using Python
11. Data optimization and data handling
12. Data organization and presentation

Leadership

With the use of technology and to meet market demands, accountants need to:[59]

1. Demonstrate leadership, self-awareness, emotional maturity, and social intelligence.
2. Uphold ethical standards, stimulate innovation, and support learning and development.
3. Learn, adapt to technological change, and continually develop skill set.
4. Follow high quality standards, provide accurate data and financial information, and establish clear communication methods.
5. Gain knowledge of economic markets, business strategies, organizational structures, corporate governance, risk management, and financial regulations.
6. Develop critical thinking and the ability to understand, explain, and provide solutions to problems faced by businesses.
7. Understand the global economy, politics, cultures, and markets to operate across boundaries and work with diverse teams and clients.
8. Focus on interpersonal skills to communicate, empathize with, and develop relationships with team members and clients.
9. Facilitate conflict management and respect opposing views.

While certain universities around the world are revising their academic curriculum to better prepare professional accountants, NASBA and the AICPA are using this information to develop the model of education for the CPAs of tomorrow.

CPA EVOLUTION

In recognition of these changing requirements and to meet the demands of future businesses, NASBA and AICPA have launched the *CPA Evolution* initiative. They are in the process of a complete overhaul of core academic and experiential requirements of obtaining a CPA license. The new Uniform CPA Exam is expected to be launched in 2024.[52][53]

Professional accountants will have to focus more on specializing in their disciplines with an integration of technology as never before. Auditors, tax professionals, risk managers, and consultants will have to learn how to mine new data sources, process even larger databases, use visualization and predictive analysis tools, and implement machine learning. They will also be required to play a greater role in the decision making and strategic planning of organizations.

The new CPA licensure model is a combination of Core accounting skills and a chosen Discipline. Candidates will be required to gain and demonstrate Core knowledge of accounting, auditing, taxation, and related technology necessary to provide services that are critical for safeguarding public interest and business operations.[55]

In addition, candidates will have to choose and pass one Discipline from the following:[54][51]

1. Business Analysis and Reporting (BAR)
2. Information Systems and Control (ISC)
3. Tax Compliance and Planning (TCP)

Choosing a particular discipline will not limit CPAs to that practice area but will give them broader knowledge in it. All new CPAs will have complete rights and privileges regardless of their choice.[51]

In 2020, Deloitte surveyed 2,737 IT and business executives to study how companies across various industries have adopted AI. 8% of the respondents stated that AI has already transformed their industry, 17% is that it will happen in less than a year, 36% believed it will happen within the next 3 years, 21% said it might take between 3 to 5 years, and 3% predicted that it will take more than 5 years for AI to have an impact on their industry.[61]

Based on this and other studies, organizations are on the threshold of remarkable evolution toward applying AI and ML to their processes.[62] What does this mean for the accountants, though?

As organizations become data-driven, there is increasing pressure on the accounting profession to change its 'modus operandi.' Accounting firms and service providers have consequently been implementing AI to detect errors, support audits, mine fraudulent data, guide financial planning, and improve efficiency.

The benefits of AI extend beyond simply saving labor costs. Accurate data by itself is invaluable, but fraud identification, higher output, faster decision making, and a wealth of information processing can give organizations an edge over their competition. Above all, costs of AI are decreasing with technological advancements.

Python thrives in such an environment because of its remarkably low implementation cost, versatility, portability, and learnability. Since automation is inevitable, it is critical that current and future business professionals possess knowledge of languages such as Python to meet the demands of their profession.

PYTHON IS NOT A REPLACEMENT

AI and ML has taken over the world by storm. From personal recommendations of TV shows to self-driving cars, automation and technology have become integral aspects of all that we do. But what does it mean for how business professionals do their part?

It is critical to understand that Python is not a replacement for many tools that have traditionally been used. Python helps augment processes, reduces time-spent, and helps tackle bigger challenges with relative ease. One of the most heard dilemmas is if Python will replace common software, such as SAP and Excel.

Python and Excel have different functionalities and purpose. Excel, before anything else, is a spreadsheet tool that can be used for easy manipulation of data without any knowledge of its underlying code. Python is a complete programming language that can be used to create complex programs and integrate different functionalities, and as such, requires knowledge of coding.[57]

Excel allows users to create data entries within cells (intersections of columns and rows) for calculations, present and visualize data into graphs, and manage the data to some extent. Python enables accountants to work in conjunction with Excel for higher efficiency, speed, flexibility, and portability.

The breadth of connections possible with Python allows for integration with several other software beyond spreadsheets. For instance, there are limitations to the quantities of data processing when only using Excel. Python has much broader limits. Corporations today deal with large volumes and varieties of data which can be efficiently managed, processed, and analyzed using Python. Professionals must understand that programming languages and other software are increasingly going to complement legacy software in the future.

For example, there is a vast collection of libraries available for Python programmers to achieve symbiosis between current desktop and cloud applications. Automation of tasks generally performed in Excel can be performed by various open-source Python libraries, such as openpyxl, xlwings, XlsxWriter, and Jinja. These libraries can be used to automate Excel processes while respecting the need for the underlying software.[56]

It must be noted that even though the native Visual Basic for Applications (VBA) in Excel can be used for data processing, analysis, and presentation, there are limits to its portability and scalability.[58] Python, with its libraries and flexible approach, allows professionals to overcome those hurdles and develop much more sophisticated solutions for automating work to meet the demands of large businesses.[60]

SECTION 02
FOUNDATIONAL PYTHON

CHAPTER 04 | LEARN TO CODE: THE BASICS OF PYTHON

Python is a comprehensive programming language that requires practice and perpetual learning. Complex applications of Python for specific use-cases demand in-depth knowledge of its functionalities.

I have provided a basic overview of the language in this book, but it is not an exhaustive resource. My purpose is to introduce the fundamentals of Python for you to begin your coding journey. There are plenty of resources to further develop your skills and knowledge as you continue to code and write programs to optimize business processes for yourself and your firm.

Books

1. Python for Everybody: Exploring Data in Python3 by Dr. Charles Severance
2. Automate the Boring Stuff with Python by Al Sweigart
3. Python for Data Analytics: Data Wrangling with pandas, NumPy, and IPython by Wes McKinney
4. Python Data Science Handbook: Essential Tools for Working with Data by Jake VanderPlas

Courses

1. Learn Python (www.learnpython.org)
2. Introduction to Python for Data Science by DataCamp (www.datacamp.com/courses/intro-to-python-for-data-science)
3. Python for Accountants | AccountingPy – (www.udemy.com/course/accountingpy)
4. Accounting Data Analytics with Python – (www.coursera.org/learn/accounting-data-analytics-python)

The following information is intended to help you kick start your Python learning and help you understand the basics before moving on to more sophisticated programming.

GETTING STARTED

Foremost, visit the official Python website (www.python.org) to familiarize yourself with important information about the language. The website is incredibly detailed; think of it as a one-stop-shop for virtually all your Python needs. You can download installers, review native documentation, and access 3rd-party libraries. You can also get involved with the broader community, follow current news, and even apply for jobs! This exhaustive resource should be one of the first bookmarks in the inevitable "Python" folder on your browser.

The website also offers information on the compatibility of various versions of Python with different operating systems. It is important to check your system specifications to make sure it is compatible with the version you plan to install. I suspect most installations to be Windows-based in a work setting, but it is always good to be sure.

Moving forward, it is important to understand these terms:

Module

One great thing about Python is that codes can piggyback off other codes to create powerful solutions. This tremendously helps in coding since blocks of code can be grouped together, stored as separate files, imported as needed, and used repeatedly. A *module* is any Python file (usually with a *.py* extension) that contains some code.

In the context of a periodic inventory system, for example, a module named "fifo.py" can be created to calculate Cost of Goods Sold (COGS) on a first-in, first-out basis. It can be subsequently imported into any script, perhaps one calculating operating income.

Package

A *package* is a collection of Python modules. Packages are organized a certain technical way with some additional required files, but in essence they are a way to further group Python code. A periodic inventory package may contain three modules called "fifo.py," "lifo.py," and "wght_avg.py."

Package Manager

When you install Python and related packages, your system creates space to store all of them for retrieval during development. This space is controlled by *package managers*. Package managers are responsible for "managing," including installing, tracking, updating, and deleting packages. Two of the most popular package managers are *pip* and *conda.*

pip

If you have ever installed a Python package, you are probably aware of *pip*, Python's native and pre-installed package manager. It is only compatible with Python packages and installs them as wheels or source distributions. You need to install a Python interpreter before using pip.

This package manager relies on the *virtualvenv* tool to create and manage isolated virtual environments. It also installs dependencies in a recurring serial loop. This means that package dependencies are not synchronously fulfilled and may result in broken environments. All you need to remember is that pip is the "go-to" package manager for most people, but it does not always install all dependencies automatically so should be used carefully.

conda

Conda is Anaconda's package and virtual environment manager that can be used to install packages from Anaconda Cloud and the primary Anaconda repository. Packages in conda are binaries which means there is no need for compilers to install them and they are not limited only to Python: they can come from C++, R, and other languages.

Conda allows you to directly create virtual environments with various versions of packages. It also uses a satisfiability (SAT) solver to check if all installed packages' requirements are satisfied to ensure there are no broken environments. In essence, when you install a package with conda, it ensures that you also install all required dependencies.

There are two main caveats with using conda over pip. First, pip is more popular among Python coders, so there is a larger support community; it is easier to find relevant documentation online. Second, Anaconda is heavier compared to native Python and requires more memory. Due to the many packages that are exclusive to pip but the other advantages conda presents, many programmers use both for optimal efficiency.

Virtual Environments

As you progress in your coding journey, you will likely create many solutions using multiple Python packages. As these packages continually get updated, chances are that the functionalities you used may no longer be supported. You could not update your packages at all, but you will lose out on all the latest improvements/features. This is where virtual environments come into play. Virtual Environments (VEs) are created within the *global* Python environment but function as separate ecosystems. VEs allow you to preserve the dependency requirements of your codes. Without them, you will likely face higher load times, code bricks, and other dependency issues, since packages would have to be retrieved from the global package manager each time you begin a code.

VEs help organize packages into respective frameworks for designated projects. This reduces load time, facilitates transitions of projects from one version of Python to the next, and allows you to easily publish your programs online for distribution.

INTEGRATED DEVELOPMENT ENVIRONMENT

As a programmer, you can use the native Python Shell to write your code. While it is a decent environment to practice your coding basics, it is unintuitive and lacks many features required for advanced scripts.

Over time, several Integrated Development Environments (IDEs) with additional features have been developed to extend Python's functionalities. An IDE is a program used to create software. IDEs have tools that are especially designed for software development, including a source code editor, execution and debugging tools, and a source control. Many IDEs can support languages other than Python which may result in heavier files; however, their features can help you create complex code with ease.

The best IDEs are designed to make coding easier. They allow you to save and pick up your projects midway; provide extensive debugging support; highlight keywords, variables, and other syntax; automatically format code; and run it within the same environment without switching to another program. You may find additional features, for example language help and source code control, in different IDEs.

IDEs offer advantages over basic code editors the same way Adobe Photoshop offers more intricate graphic design capabilities over MS Paint, or how Microsoft Word offers wider text processing capabilities over Notepad.

I recommend you use basic code editors only to practice code writing and experiment with various features of Python programming. For broader projects, install and use an IDE that best suits your project requirements. There are many options to choose from, but I discuss the ones I use the most.

IDLE

Python's Integrated Development and Learning Environment (IDLE) comes pre-installed with Python. It offers a basic albeit interactive interpreter with highlighting, debugging, and auto-completion features. IDLE is well suited for small, simple projects; however, I do not recommend it for larger, more complex ones.

Jupyter Notebook

Jupyter is a browser-based, interactive Python IDE that is useful for running and combining codes, visualizing data, and creating notebook documents where you can run codes cell-by-cell. Perhaps Jupyter's chief selling point is its notebook-based environment. This allows for systematic programming within a very clean, intuitive interface. Jupyter's construct makes it arguably the best Python IDE for instructional/educational purposes. It also supports HTML formatting.

Spyder

Spyder is ideal for intensive results-based coding and scientific development. It offers many useful features such as an interactive shell, autocompletion, code linting, and debugging. Based on my experience, Spyder does not have a very "clean" UI (unlike Jupyter), but offers strong support for fast, seamless coding. In addition to cell-based execution, Spyder allows for selecting and running partial code. This functionality is extremely helpful for grouping and testing chunks of code, especially during debugging.

PyCharm

PyCharm is a full-feature IDE best suited for professional developers. It has a basic free version and a paid version with complete features and web development support. While it is excellent for seasoned programmers, it is not ideal for beginners and requires more computing power than other IDEs. I have rarely found a need for developing in PyCharm.

ANACONDA

As discussed, many IDEs are available to write code. Since IDEs are often designed for specific purposes, it is often cumbersome to install/uninstall them as per your requirements. Using different IDEs also means that you need to install all dependencies correctly, increasing the potential for errors. A simple solution to avoid so much hassle is to use the Anaconda distribution.

Anaconda is a Python and R distribution, package manager, and virtual environment manager. It comes with over 7,500 data science and machine learning packages. Its open-source ecosystem is used by over 25 million people worldwide and, as such, it offers a massive support community.

Conda (introduced earlier) can be used to maintain multiple virtual environments simultaneously. Anaconda comes with a GUI (graphical user interface) program called the Anaconda Navigator to launch many popular IDEs, including Jupyter, RStudio, Spyder, or VSCode. It includes a myriad of pre-installed packages such as NumPy and pandas.

I highly recommend installing Anaconda. This ensures that all Python dependencies are correctly installed. This also helps in seamlessly switching between IDEs based on need or personal preference.

Installing Anaconda

There are various methods available to install Python, including package managers, specialized distributions, embedded systems, and official Python distributions. I am going to stick with the Anaconda distribution for Windows.

Visit the official Anaconda website and download the Anaconda Individual Edition on your computer. Once the file has finished downloading, open and run the installer. Go with the latest version of Python unless you have specific reason not to.

Step 1

Click the 'Next' button on the installer's welcome screen.

Step 2

Read the License Agreement and click on the 'I Agree' button.

Step 3

I recommend installing Anaconda for an individual user where you do not require administrator permissions to run the program. On this screen, select 'Just Me' and click 'Next.' You may nevertheless require admin permissions if you are installing on your work computer.

Step 4

Check your installation location. You can change the location as per your preference, but make sure you have enough space available on your computer. Click 'Next.'

Step 5

The installer will ask you to choose whether to add Anaconda to PATH. I recommend that you leave this unchecked for technical reasons I will not delve into.

Step 6

Click on 'Install' and wait for Anaconda to finish installing.

Step 7

On the next screen, you will be asked if you want to install Microsoft Visual Studio Code. Decide as per need. Click 'Next.'

Step 8

This is the final screen. You have successfully installed Anaconda on your system and can now begin writing your first Python program. Check both boxes on this screen to learn more about Anaconda and how to get started. Click 'Finish' and you're all set.

DEVELOPING WITH PYTHON

SYNTAX

Originally developed by Guido van Rossum, Python was released in 1991 and quickly became a popular programming language because of its ease-of-use and relatively uncomplicated syntax. Syntax refers to the rules-set that defines the structure of a programming language and consequently dictates writing and interpretation. The Python syntax includes several items of consideration:

Identifiers

These are used to identify variables, objects, modules, functions, classes, etc. Think of an identifier as the "name" given anything that needs to be uniquely referenced. Identifiers can contain letters, digits, or an underscore (_). However, they cannot start with a digit. Python does not allow the use of other symbols, such as $ or #, in identifiers. Consider the following:

- Python is case-sensitive. "Invoice_List" and "invoice_list" are two separate identifiers.
- "1frame" is not a valid identifier. "frame1" is a valid identifier.
- "_data" is a valid identifier. However, by convention, identifiers beginning with an underscore are meant for internal use by the developer only.
- "__data" is also valid, but double underscores are very rarely used to begin an identifier.

Reserved Words

Certain words are reserved in Python. They already have an established meaning within the Python ecosystem and cannot be used as identifiers. Currently, there are 33 reserved words:

1. and
2. as
3. assert
4. break
5. class
6. continue
7. def
8. del
9. elif
10. else
11. except
12. False
13. finally
14. for
15. from

16. global
17. if
18. import
19. in
20. is
21. lambda
22. None
23. nonlocal
24. not
25. or
26. pass
27. raise
28. return
29. True
30. try
31. while
32. with
33. yield

Operators

Operators are symbols used to perform specific operations. They perform arithmetic and logical computations. The variable on which the operator operates is called the *operand*. There are seven types of operators in Python.

1. **Arithmetic**
   These are used with numeric values for mathematical operations.

Operator	Name
+	Addition
-	Subtraction
*	Multiplication
/	Division
%	Modulus
**	Exponentiation
//	Floor division

2. **Bitwise**
   These operators work bitwise and help compare binary numbers by operating on operands as strings of binary digits. They are not commonly used, except in set theory.

Operator	Name
&	AND
|	OR
~	NOT

^	XOR
>>	Right shift
<<	Left shift

3. **Membership**

   These are used to check whether a value or variable is present in a sequence or a collection.

Operator	Meaning
in	True when variable is present
not in	True when value is not present

4. **Identity**

   These are used to test and compare the presence of identical objects in the same memory location. Two equal values or variables are not necessarily identical.

Operator	Meaning
is	True when objects are identical
is not	True when objects are not identical

5. **Comparison**

   These are used to compare two values and result in a Boolean output.

Operator	Name
>	Greater than
<	Less than
==	Equal to
!=	Not equal to

>=	Greater than or equal to
<=	Less than or equal to

6. **Assignment**

These operators are used to assign a specific value to a variable. Compound assignment operators update the operand to a new value by performing operations on its current value.

Operator	**Equivalence**
=	a = 8
+=	a = a + 8
-=	a = a – 8
*=	a = a * 8
/=	a = a / 8
%=	a = a % 8
//=	a = a // 8
**=	a = a ** 8
&=	a = a & 8
|=	a = a | 8
^=	a = a ^ 8
>>=	a = a >> 8
<<=	a = a << 8

7. **Logical**

These are used for multiple statements and return a Boolean output.

Operator	**Meaning**
and	True when all statements are true
or	True when either statement is true
not	Inverts resulting Boolean value

Indentation

In Python, indentation (space at the beginning of a code) is used to control the order of execution and separate different blocks of code. Code chunks with equal indents are interpreted as occurring at the same "level." This is sometimes referred to as the *off-side* rule. As your code increases in length and complexity, especially with loops included, paying attention to indentation becomes important.

```
if 10 < 15:
        print("Ten is less than fifteen")
```

Output: Ten is less than fifteen

You can use as much space as you want to create an indentation, but you must add at least one space. You must also maintain consistent spacing at the same level to avoid a syntax error. Most IDEs automatically add indents after a loop or a conditional is initiated. A common practice is to use tabs instead of spaces for uniformity and convenience.

```
if 10 < 15:
        print ("Ten is less than Fifteen")
          print("Done!")
```

Output: IndentationError: unexpected indent

Spaces

While you must maintain a specific indent in each block of code for it to be executed properly, spaces within the same line are a personal preference. These are spaces you add between characters of your code. You can use as much spacing as you like to improve legibility. For instance, *print(x)* is the same as *print (x)* or *print (x)*.

Comments

Comments are used for annotating code in Python. They help the reader understand the purpose of some code. Use comments to make your notes as you code. Comments are ignored during execution.

Single line comments can be added using a hash (#).

```
if 10 < 15:
        print("Ten is less than fifteen")              # Indented within
conditional
```

Output: Ten is less than fifteen

Python does not have a dedicated multi-line comment mechanism. The recommended way to create multi-line comments is to add a # in front of each line. Sometimes strings are used as comments.

```
if 10 < 15:                                            # Multi-line comment
        print("Ten is less than Fifteen")              # continued here
```

Output: Ten is less than fifteen

Order of Execution

Python code is executed sequentially, from top to bottom. Consider this example: the value of *y* does not update with a subsequent update to *x*.

```
x = 5
y = x
x = 6

print(y)
```

Output: 5

VARIABLES

Variables are the most common type of identifiers. They are unique in that they are used to allocate memory to and store values. You can assign values to variables using the simple assignment operator (=). A value here refers to a traditional value (e.g., 8), a function, a sequence, or anything else that can be stored in memory.

Variable Names

You can use either a short variable name, such as "a" or "b" or a descriptive one, such as "animal" or "meals."

```
vendors = ["abc co", "xyz inc", "123 llp"]
num_accounts = 8
```

The rules for assigning variable names are much the same as those for identifiers:

1. Start the name with either a letter or an underscore
2. Do not start the name with a number
3. Names can only contain alphanumeric characters and underscores
4. Names are case-sensitive (Loss, loss, and LOSS are all different variables)

Creating Variables

There is no specific command for creating a variable; use of the simple assignment operator (=) applies most frequently.

```
a = 8
b = 9
print(a, "+", b, "=",  a+b)        # prints text in console
```

Output: 8 + 9 = 17

Defining Data Type

Python does not require you to declare the data type of a variable at assignment. This is one of the big benefits of Python: it automatically defines data type based on input characteristics. Additionally, data types can be changed at any time.

```
a = "Accounting"        # a is automatically assigned type str
b = 8                   # b is automatically assigned type int
b + a
```

Output: TypeError: unsupported operand type(s) for +: 'int' and 'str'

Casting

While Python can automatically assign variable type at execution, situations inevitably arise where you need to declare the variable type explicitly. Casting can be used to define specific data types for variables. It can also be used to convert one data type into another, assuming conversion is possible.

```
a = str(123456)         #a will be '123456'
b = int("8")            #b will be 8
c = float(b)            #c will be 8.0
```

Getting the Data Type

The *type()* function can be used to get the data type of a variable.

```
a = "Accounting"
b = 8
c = ("Accounting", 8)
print(type(a))
print(type(b))
print(type(c))
```

Output: <class 'str'>
<class 'int'>
<class 'tuple'>

Declaring String Variables

Single or double quotes can be used to define strings. I use double quotes, but that is just my personal preference. I alternate between single and double quotes throughout the book.

```
a = "Accounting"
# is the same as
a = 'Accounting'
```

Assigning Multiple Values

You can assign multiple values to multiple variables, a single value to multiple variables, or create a collection of variables in a single line.

```
a, b, c = "Goodwill", "Trademark", "Patent"
                                        # Multiple values to multiple variables
print(a, b, c)
```

Output: Goodwill Trademark Patent

```
a = b = c = "Goodwill"          # Single value to multiple variables
a == b == c
```

Output: True

```
intangibles = ["Goodwill", "Trademark", "Patent"]       # List of strings
a, b, c = intangibles      # Known as "Unpacking"
print(a)
print(b)
print(c)
```

Output: Goodwill
Trademark
Patent

DATA TYPES

Python variables can store values of several data types. Each data type comes with its own sets of limitation, features, and good-to-knows. As mentioned before, the *type()* function can be used to determine the data type of a variable.

Python includes a range of built-in data types; however, there are many user-created types as well.

1. Numeric

Numeric data types are based on numeric values. They are further divided into three categories:

a. Integer
These include whole numbers, without any fractions or decimals, as positive or negative values. Integers are defined by the *int* class. Python has no limitations on the length of an integer value.

b. Float
Real numbers with a floating point are called float. Floats are represented by a decimal point. They are defined by the *float* class. You can add the irrational constant "e"/"E" to indicate scientific notation. Floats are accurate up to 15 decimal points by default; any values with more than 15 decimals are automatically truncated.

c. Complex Numbers
These constitute a combination of a real number and an imaginary number. Defined by the *complex* class, they are written as "a+bj". I doubt you will ever use this data type.

```
x = 8
print ("Type of x: ", type(x))

y = 3.2
print ("Type of y: ", type(y))

z = 4 + 7j
print ("Type of z: ", type(z))
```

Output: Type of x: <class 'int'>
Type of y: <class 'float'>
Type of z: <class 'complex'>

2. Boolean

Defined by the *bool* class, Boolean objects are binary; they are either *True* or *False*. The first letter must be uppercase to denote Boolean values. Expressions can be determined as True or False in a Boolean context.

True values are often called "truthy," while false values are referred to as "falsy."

```
print(3/2 > 5)              # Expression evaluating to a Boolean value
print(type(True))
print(type(False))
print(type(true))
```

Output: False
<class 'bool'>
<class 'bool'>
NameError: name 'true' is not defined

3. Sequences

Sequences are used to efficiently store multiple values in a single variable. Whenever you want to work with a group of items, you can turn to sequences. Although conventionally created to store ordered data, sequences can also be used to store unordered values (I frequently use them). There are three types of sequences:

a. String

The technical definition: Unicode characters represented by arrays of bytes are called strings. What you need to know: if you work with text, you will probably use strings. Defined by the *str* class, strings are a collection of characters written inside single, double, or triple quotation marks.

Strings are important! As a business professional, you likely work with a lot of textual data. Bank statements, company filings, vendor invoices, journal entries, etc., are all filled with text. Strings are unique in that they are very often used in conjunction with other sequences (it is common to have strings inside a list, but not a tuple inside a list). Be sure you thoroughly understand strings; this will empower you to create very sophisticated solutions. Consult other resources as needed.

```
String1 = 'Accounting Ledger'
print('String1 is', String1, ', and it is in single quotes')

String2 = "Company's Financial Records"
print("String2 is", String2, ", and it is in double quotes")

String3 = '''Crypto
          Investments'''
print('''Multi-line String3 is''', String3, ''', and it is in triple quotes''')
```

Output: String1 is Accounting Ledger, and it is in single quotes
String2 is Company's Financial Records, and it is in double quotes
Multi-line
String3 is Crypto Investments, and it is in triple quotes

b. List

Lists are one of the most used sequences in Python. Lists are highly flexible since the underlying items do not have to be of the same data type. Additionally, they are mutable, allowing for the manipulation of the contents' values and other characteristics.

For most collections you encounter, you will probably want to work with lists. This is because you can overwrite/update a list's contents, and I have found it necessary for most tasks. To create a list, separate each item with a comma and place inside square brackets ([]). Also, note that lists, like most iterables in Python, are 0-indexed (explained later).

```
x = [2, 4, 6, 8, 10, 12, 14, 16]
print(x[2])
x[3] = "text"              # Lists are mutable
print(x)
```

Output: 6
[2, 4, 6, 'text', 10, 12, 14, 16]

c. Tuple

The major difference between lists and tuples is that tuples are immutable: once created, they cannot be manipulated. Tuples are generally created for write-protected data. Use tuples if you have ordered data that should not be changed after creation (for example, specific employee information that doesn't change). Tuples are generally faster to generate because Python does not need to allocate extra memory for possible updates.

Tuples are created by separating each item with a comma and then placing them inside parentheses ().

```
t = (8, 'accounts', 4+3j)

print(t[1])
print(t[0:3])
t[0] = 12          # Generates error. Tuples are immutable
```

Output: accounts
(8, 'accounts', 4+3j)
TypeError: 'tuple' object does not support item assignment

4. Unordered Collections

Unordered collections in Python are powerful data types. If order is not important, these collections can provide a plethora of useful features that sequences do not. I use two types regularly:

a. Set

Sets are unordered, iterable, deduplicated, and mutable collections. Although the order of elements is undefined, sets can contain heterogenous data types. Sets are created using the *set()* function. They are modeled on the mathematical set theory and support corresponding operations like unions and intersections.

There are two key points to remember for sets: first, sets are always deduplicated. They automatically drop any duplicate values even if the user passes them. This feature can be very handy when you wish to deduplicate a group of values. Second, sets are unordered but mutable.

Because they are unordered, you cannot access an item within a set with an index (unlike sequences). You can, however, add or delete items by explicitly passing the value itself.

```
set1 = set()
print("First Blank Set")
print(set1)

# Set from a string
set2 = set("RecordsForAudit")
print("\nSet with the use of String")
print(set2)

# Set from a list
set3 = set(["Records", "For", "Audit"])
print("\nSet with the use of List")
print(set3)

# Set with mixed type of values
set4 = set([1, 2, 2, 4, 'Records', 4, 'For', 6, 'Audit']) # Observe duplicates
print("\nSet with the use of Mixed Values")
print(set4)
```

Output: First Blank Set
set()

Set with the use of String
{'F', 'o', 'R', 's', 'r', 'c', 'd', 'A', 'u', 'i', 't'}

Set with the use of List
{'Records', 'For', 'Audit'}

Set with the use of Mixed Values
{1, 2, 4, 6, 'Records', 'For', 'Audit'}

b. Dictionary

Python allows for storage of data as an unordered collection of key-value pairs (collectively known as items). Each key is separated from its value by a colon (:), and key-value pairs are separated by a comma (,).

Dictionaries are defined using curly brackets ({}) but can also be created using the built-in function *dict()*.

While values can belong to any data type and can be updated/repeated, keys are immutable and deduplicated. Remember, both sets and dictionaries use curly brackets as containers. However, empty sets can only be created using the *set()* function, whereas empty dictionaries can be created just by passing empty curly brackets.

```
# An empty Dictionary
dict1 = dict()                    # Could also use {}
print("Empty dictionary")
print(dict1)

# Dictionary with Integer Keys
dict2 = {1: 'Records', 2: 'For', 3: 'Audit'}
print("\nDictionary with integer keys")
print(dict2)

# Dictionary with Mixed keys & values
dict3 = {'Name': 'Accounts', 1: [1, 2, 3, 4]}
print("\nDictionary with mixed keys & values")
print(dict3)

# Dictionary from a list using dict()
dict4 = dict([(1, 'Records'), (2, 'For')])
print("\nDictionary from a list using dict()")
print(dict4)
```

Output: Empty dictionary

{}

Dictionary with integer keys

{1: 'Records', 2: 'For', 3: 'Audit'}

Dictionary with the use of Mixed Keys

{1: [1, 2, 3, 4], 'Name': 'Accounts'}

Dictionary from a list using dict()

{1: 'Records', 2: 'For', 3: 'Audit'}

Since dictionaries optimize data retrieval, it is important to know how to access values in them. You do this by using a value's key inside square brackets, or by using the *get()* function.

```
# Creating a Dictionary
dict1 = {1: 'Records', 'name': 'for', 3: 'Audit'}

# Accessing an element using a key
print("Accessing an element using a key:")
print(dict1['name'])

# Accessing an element using get() method
print("\nAccessing an element using get:")
print(dict1.get(3))
```

Output: Accessing an element using a key:
for

Accessing an element using get:
Audit

CONDITIONALS

Conditional statements provide Python with rules for decision making. They provide a set of Boolean expressions, each followed by some code. The code executed is nested in the first expression that evaluates to True.

Virtually all coding solutions use conditionals. There is almost always at least one decision making point. Conditionals cease after the first True evaluation is achieved and the corresponding code is executed.

1. if

if consists of a Boolean expression followed by one or more statements.

```
a= 5
if (a < 10):      # () can be used for clarity
        print(a, "is less than 10")
```

Output: 5 is less than 10

2. if-elif-else

if can be followed by optional *elif* and *else* statements. *elif* is used to provide multiple conditions. *else* is meant to be a "catch-all" expression that executes only when no other condition is True. A python program simply moves on from a conditional statement when no condition evaluates to True and an *else* statement is not included.

```
x = 34/5
if x < 5:
        print(x, "is smaller than 5")
elif 5 <= x <= 7:
        print(x, "is between 5 and 7")
else:
        print(x, "is greater than 7")
```

Output: 6.8 is between 5 and 7

Nested Conditionals

You can use conditionals inside other conditionals to handle more complicated operations.

Under current IRS rules, a corporation receiving dividends from another corporation can deduct from income all or part of those dividends, depending on how "affiliated" the two entities are. Affiliation is usually measured by common ownership. The deduction is known as the Dividends Received Deduction.

```
# Assume variables "company_type" & "ownership_percent" exist

if company_type == "c-corp":
        if ownership_percent < .20:
                drd = .50
        elif ownership_percent > .80:
                drd = 1
        else:
                drd = .65
```

LOOPS

Loops allow you to execute code multiple times. If you have code that you need to run for multiple values, you can use a loop instead of repeating the code.

Together with conditionals, loops can tackle almost any task! Code for most tasks will include at least one loop, be it scanning documents, downloading invoices, parsing images, etc.

Iterable

Loops rely on the underlying concept of iterables. An iterable is any object in Python that can be worked on successively, one value at a time. All sequences and collections are iterables. Some iterables, such as a string, explicitly display their contents (e.g., "python" consists of "p", "y", "t", "h", "o", "n"). Other iterables, such as *range()* objects, are not explicit and must be looped over to display content.

There are two types of loops you need to know.

1. for

for loops are used for looping over an iterable. They are, in my opinion, the most important and commonly used loops in Python.

The stopping criterion for a *for* loop is the length of the iterable; they run until all values in the iterable are looped over. Think of a *for* loop as: "You have a collection of x items. Continue running this code x times, one for each item in the list."

```
# List containing depreciation methods
depr_methods = ["SL", "DDB", "MACRS", "UOP"]
for method in depr_methods:
        print(method)
```

Output: SL
DDB
MACRS
UOP

2. while

while loops continue until a certain Boolean condition is met. This stopping criterion may cause a *while* loop to terminate before all items in an iterable have been looped over.

Think of a *while* loop as: "You have a collection of x items. Until a specific condition is met, continue to run the loop. If the condition is met, stop the loop. If the condition is never met, continue until all items have been looped over."

```
n = 1
while n <= 10:
        print(n)
        n += 1          # Alias for n = n + 1
print("The program has ended since n is now greater than 10")
```

Output: *1*
2
3
4
5
6
7
8
9
10
The program has ended since n is now greater than 10

Infinite Loops

Infinite loops are exactly what their name suggests: they run indefinitely! Their stopping criterion is usually external to your script (memory issue, power failure, malware, etc.).

Infinite loops can be useful in certain situations. They can be justified when, for example, a main server code needs to continuously run until the IT team decides to shut the server down. However, they are very easy to create inadvertently, almost always with the *while* loop. Always exercise caution to not create an infinite loop by mistake.

In the below example, the loop will continue indefinitely because of the easily committable oversight of not incrementing i. Observe that the code is technically correct.

```
i=0
while i <= 10:
        text = "Why is this not ending?"
```

Nested Loops

As with conditionals, loops can be created within other loops. Remember, nested loops are tricky. It is easy to get lost in the complexities of multiple loops. In a 2-loop nest, the outer loop controls the overall iteration in the code: for each item of the outer iterable, the inner loop is executed completely. For example, if the outer iterable has 6 items and the inner iterable has 4 items, a total of 24 iterations are executed.

```
assets = [["Cash", "Inventory", "AR"], ["PPE", "Land", "NR"]]
asset_type = "Current Asset"
for asset_list in assets:
        for asset in asset_list:
                print(asset, "is a", asset_type)
        print("\n")        # Newline character prints a blank line
        asset_type = "Fixed Asset"
```

Output: Cash is a Current Asset
Inventory is a Current Asset
AR is a Current Asset

PPE is a Fixed Asset
Land is a Fixed Asset
NR is a Fixed Asset

continue, break

These two statements are used to alter the execution of a loop. The *continue* statement ignores part of the loop that occurs after it and returns execution to the start of the loop for the next item. The *break* statement completely terminates the loop; the program cuts out of the loop and moves on. In a nested loop, *continue* and *break* apply only to the innermost loop that contains them.

```
for val in "string":
        print(val)
        if val == "i":
                break
print("the end")
```

Output: s
t
r
the end

```
for val in "string":
        if val == "i":
                continue
        print(val)
print("the end")
```

Output: s
t
r
n
g
the end

ERROR HANDLING

Errors are any problems in a program that may halt its execution. Several of the examples before returned errors because of incorrect coding. As you continue your coding journey, you will realize that errors are an inevitability in programming. As code becomes more complex, the risk of errors can be mitigated but not avoided.

Two broad types of errors occur in Python:

1. Syntax Errors

If the syntax of a code block or program is "illegal" (often used in Python context), the program will terminate and throw a Syntax Error. These errors occur when you make a structural error in your Python code. For example, forgetting to close a string with a quote will result in this error.

2. Exceptions

Your program can have no syntax issues and still result in an error. Exceptions occur because of some logical fallacy in the code, even if it is syntactically correct. Trying to divide by 0 is an exception, as is trying to loop over a numeric object.

You are on your own with syntax errors; the best way to avoid them is to learn and not repeat! However, there is no way to foresee all exceptions that could occur. Exceptions can be handled using the *try* statement and the *except*, *else*, and *finally* clauses.

a. try-except

This is the basic combination used to test a code block for potential exceptions. Code with potential exceptions is placed inside the *try* statement, while code that handles the exceptions is placed inside the *except* clause.

The quick ratio is an indicator of a company's ability to meet liabilities through immediately liquid assets. It excludes inventory. The following code throws an error because the last tuple contains a string.

```
# Nested tuple grouped as (current assets, inventory, current liabilities)
values = ((50000, 10000, 30000), (30250, 5100, 40500), (20154, 0,
'25000'))
```

```
for group in values:
        quick_ratio = round((group[0] - group[1])/group[2], 2)
        print(quick_ratio)
```

Output: 1.33
0.62
TypeError: unsupported operand type(s) for /: 'int' and 'str'

Compare the above to the following code.

```
values = ((50000, 10000, 30000), (30250, 5100, 40500), (20154, 0,
'25000'))
for group in values:
        try:
                quick_ratio = round((group[0] - group[1])/ group[2], 2)
                print(quick_ratio)
                except:
                        print("There is some issue. Check numbers")
```

Output: 1.33
0.62
There is some issue. Check numbers

b. else

This is an optional clause that is executed only if the *try* statement is successful, i.e., if there are no errors. It will be ignored if the program must move to the *except* clause.

```
values = ((50000, 10000, 30000), (30250, 5100, 40500), (20154, 0,
'25000'))
for group in values:
        try:
                quick_ratio = round((group[0] - group[1])/ group[2], 2)
        except:
                print("There is some issue. Check numbers")
        else:
                print("No error. Quick ratio:", quick_ratio)
```

Output: No error. Quick ratio: 1.33
No error. Quick ratio: 0.62
There is some issue. Check numbers

c. finally

This clause is also optional. It gets executed regardless of if the *try* clause is successful or if the code moves to the *except* clause.

```
values = ((50000, 10000, 30000), (30250, 5100, 40500), (20154, 0,
'25000'))
for group in values:
        try:
                quick_ratio = round((group[0] - group[1])/ group[2], 2)
        except:
                        print("There is some issue. Check numbers")
                else:
                        print("No error. Quick ratio:", quick_ratio)

        finally:
                        print("Done with this one!")
```

Output: No error. Quick ratio: 1.33
Done with this one!
No error. Quick ratio: 0.62
Done with this one!
There is some issue. Check numbers
Done with this one!

d. raise

This can be used to force a particular exception to occur. A single *raise* argument at the end is used to indicate the exception you want to raise. I have never had to use this clause.

```
try:
        10/0
except:
        print ("Still raising an error")
        raise
```

Output: ZeroDivisionError: division by zero

Python allows programmers to be pro-active and test code block-by-block before execution. A faulty program with errors will crash and pose obvious challenges. Several IDEs, such as Spyder and PyCharm, come with in-built debugging and verification options to ease the error handling process for you. Remember, strategic use of error handling often differentiates a great programmer from a good one.

FUNCTIONS

A function is a pre-written, organized, reusable block of code that is used to perform actions. Python provides several built-in functions like *print()*, etc. You can also create your own functions.

Functions are not always necessary. But, like *try-except* blocks, they are used by great programmers to make their code clean, intuitive, and replicable. In analytical fields such as accounting, functions can make lives much easier! You can create functions for calculations that you do regularly, including ratio analysis, financial metrics, audit risks, sampling, tax computations, etc.

Creating a Function

In Python, a function is created using the *def* keyword. The in-built *input()* function allows the user to enter information at execution, so it helps in making other functions more dynamic.

The audit risk model defines audit risk as product of the inherently present risk of an engagement, the risk of internal control failure, and the auditor-specified acceptable risk that a material misstatement will go undetected. In practice, the auditor sets an acceptable detection risk based on the level of inherent and control risks so as to mitigate the overall audit risk.

```
def acceptable_detection_risk():
        IR = input("Please input Inherent Risk: ").lower()
        CR = input("Please input Control Risk: ").lower()

        if IR == "high" and CR == "high":
                print("Acceptable Detection Risk is LOW")
        elif IR == "low" and CR == "low":
                print("Acceptable Detection Risk is HIGH")
        else:
                print("Acceptable Detection Risk is MEDIUM")
```

Calling a Function

After creating a function, you can call it by using its name followed by the parentheses containing any required arguments.

```
# Call a function
acceptable_detection_risk()
```

Output: Please input Inherent Risk: high
Please input Control Risk: high
Acceptable Detection Risk is LOW

Arguments

Arguments are values passed inside the parentheses of the function. Arguments can be required or optional. Positional order is important. The number of arguments in a function call should match the number in the function definition. Arguments can be defined with default values at creation, in which case they need not be provided at execution unless a different value needs to be passed. The previous example can also be written without the *input()* function, and required values can be passed as arguments.

```
def acceptable_detection_risk(IR, CR):
        if IR == "high" and CR == "high":
                print("Acceptable Detection Risk is LOW")
        elif IR == "low" and CR == "low":
                print("Acceptable Detection Risk is HIGH")
        else:
                print("Acceptable Detection Risk is MEDIUM")
```

```
acceptable_detection_risk(IR = "high", CR = "low")
```

Output: Acceptable Detection Risk is MEDIUM

```
acceptable_detection_risk("low", "low") # implicit positional inference
```

Output: Acceptable Detection Risk is HIGH

return

It is very important to distinguish between the *print()* and *return* statements. A function can provide results with both these statements. However, the *return* statement sends output back to the caller, while the *print()* statement simply displays the output at execution. You can therefore use *return* to assign the function's output to a variable. This can be very useful if you need to use the output elsewhere in the code. A *return* statement does not require parentheses.

```
def simple_interest_print(p, r, t):
        print((p * r * t)/100)
si = simple_interest_print(500, 5, 2)    # Assign function to a variable
si/10                                    # Call variable
```

Output: 50.0

TypeError: unsupported operand type(s) for /: 'NoneType' and 'int'

```
def simple_interest_ret(p, r, t):
        return (p * r * t)/100
si = simple_interest_ret(500, 5, 2)      # Assign function to a variable
si/10                                    # Call variable
```

Output: 5.0

CHAPTER 05 | **MORE ON PYTHON**

KEY PROGRAMMING CONCEPTS

ATTRIBUTES VS. METHODS

Object-oriented programming languages like Python have classes made up of attributes and methods. An attribute defines a particular characteristic of an object of the class. A method, on the other hand, is a function that manipulates the class object in some way. To differentiate between the two, remember that methods usually contain parentheses whereas attributes do not.

```
import pandas as pd

frame = pd.read_csv(file_path)          # Import csv file

# Attribute
frame.columns                    # Returns the column names in a list

# Method
frame.concat(another_frame)          # Concatenates two dataframes
```

MORE DETAILS ON SEQUENCES

Indexing

Sequences are ordered. They have a specific place, or "index," assigned to each element they contain. Using these indices, you can access individual items within a sequence. Indexing is a vital concept and is one of the most prominent benefits that sequences enjoy over unordered collections.

In python, all sequences (and most iterables) are *0-indexed* from the left. For example, "b" has an index value of 0 and "g" of 10 in the string "bookkeeping".

From the right, however, indices are negative and begin with -1. For the same sequence, "g" has an index value of -1 and "b" has an index value of -11. Depending on circumstances, you may choose to access an element from either side using the appropriate index.

```
alph_str = "abcdefgh"
alph_list_rev = ["h", "g", "f", "e", "d", "c", "b", "a"]

print(alph_str[0] == alph_list_rev[-1])
print(alph_str[3] == alph_str[-5] == "d")
alph_list_rev[1] = 1            # Replace item in list, a mutable sequence
print(alph_list_rev)
```

Output: True
True
['h', 1, 'f', 'e', 'd', 'c', 'b', 'a']

Slicing Sequences

The power of indexing is evident in slicing. Slicing is used to make a "slice," or access a range of items, in a sequence. If the sequence is mutable, you can also delete or replace the group of items. Slicing can be performed using both positive (left) and negative (right) indices.

Mastering slicing is critical to developing advanced and useful codes. You may build an automation, for example, to download vendor invoices, rename them, and then scan them for amounts. Slicing will allow you to extract specific amounts from the swamp of textual information and unwanted characters rendered using OCR. It will also allow you to rename the downloaded invoices appropriately (e.g., remove "LLP" from vendor names).

The *slice()* function is used to slice sequences. Although the function can be used with an explicit call, it is more commonly called implicitly using colons (:). Indices may be provided from the left, right, or a combination of the two.

```
# Slice syntax
sequence[slice(start, stop, step)]
```

```
# Equivalent
sequence[start:stop:step]
```

- *start* indicates the slice's beginning. It defaults to 0 in the absence of a specified index (remember, sequences are 0-indexed). The slice is inclusive of the *start* value.
- *stop* indicates the slice's end. It defaults to the last position in the absence of a specified index. The slice is exclusive of the *stop* value.
- *step* indicates the slice's increment. It defaults to 1 in the absence of a specified value, which picks all values between *start* and *stop*. A step index of 2 results in the slice picking every other value.

```
num_list = []
for num in range(10):
        num_list.append(num)

print("Original List:", num_list)
print(num_list[0:5] == num_list[:5] == [0, 1, 2, 3, 4])
print(num_list[:4])              # From left
print(num_list[-5:-4])           # From right
print(num_list[-6:9:2])          # Combination
print(num_list[::-1])            # Negative step reverses sequence
```

Output: Original List: [0, 1, 2, 3, 4, 5, 6, 7, 8, 9]
True
[0, 1, 2, 3]
[5]
[4, 6, 8]
[9, 8, 7, 6, 5, 4, 3, 2, 1, 0]

String Methods

There are several string methods. Remember, strings are important! They form the basis for working with textual data in Python. While there are many methods, I use some more often than others.

```
# Assume company name scanned from an invoice
myco = "    $Company Name$   an_unnecessarily_long_name, llc"

print("Uncleaned -", myco)
split_str = myco.split()
```

```
split_str[0] = split_str[0].strip("$") + " " + split_str[1].strip("$") + ":"
split_str.remove(split_str[1])
split_str[1] = split_str[1].replace("_", " ").title()
split_str[2] = split_str[2].upper()

myco_cln = " ".join(split_str)

print("Cleaned -", myco_cln)
```

Output: Uncleaned - $Company Name$ an_unnecessarily_long_name, llc
Cleaned - Company Name: An Unnecessarily Long Name, LLC

Some commonly used string methods follow. Note that none of the methods will update the existing string because strings are immutable. Be sure to consult official Python documentation for the complete and most updated list.

String Method	Definition
lower()	Returns the string in lowercase
upper()	Returns the string in uppercase
islower()	Returns True if the entire string is lowercase
isupper()	Returns True if the entire string is uppercase
swapcase()	Swaps case from upper to lower and vice-versa
title()	Returns the string in title case (each word's 1st letter capitalized)
capitalize()	Returns the string with the 1st letter of only the 1st word capitalized
count()	Returns the count of a specified substring in the string
find()	Returns the starting index of a specified substring's 1st instance in the string. Returns -1 if not found
index()	Returns the starting index of a specified substring's 1st instance in the string. Raises exception if not found
rfind()	Returns the starting index of a specified substring's last instance in the string. Returns -1 if not found

rindex()	Returns the starting index of a specified substring's last instance in the string. Raises exception if not found
strip()	Truncates leading and trailing instances of a specified character(s) in the string. Defaults to truncating whitespaces
lstrip()	Truncates leading instances of specified character(s) in the string. Defaults to truncating whitespaces
rstrip()	Truncates trailing instances of specified character(s) in the string. Defaults to truncating whitespaces
split()	Splits the string from left on specified character(s) up to an optionally specified maximum times. Returns list
rsplit()	Splits the string from left on specified character(s) up to an optionally specified maximum times. Equivalent to *split()* unless maximum times specified
replace()	Replaces a specified substring in the string with another substring
splitlines()	Splits the string at line breaks. Equivalent to *split("\n")*
startswith()	Returns True if the string begins with a specified substring
endswith()	Returns True if the string ends with a specified substring

List Methods

Although strings are technically the broadest, they are not "sequences" in the traditional sense. You cannot store your arrays in strings. Because of their mutability, lists should be your default choice to store serial data unless there is reason to go otherwise.

```
py_list = [8, 4, 6, 7, 3, 2, 1, 1]

py_list.append(5)
print(py_list)
print(py_list.index(6))
py_list.sort(reverse = True)          # Sort descending
print(py_list)
```

Output: [8, 4, 6, 7, 3, 2, 1, 1, 5]
2
[8, 7, 6, 5, 4, 3, 2, 1, 1]

Here are some commonly used list methods. Some methods will update the existing list; others will return a new list and/or value.

List Method	Definition
append()	Adds an element at the end of the list
insert()	Adds an element at a specified index value in the list
extend()	Adds all elements of one list at the end of another
remove()	Removes an element from the list
pop()	Removes and returns an element from the list
index()	Returns the index of a specified item's 1st match from the list
sort()	Sorts the list's elements in ascending order (unless reverse is set to True)
reverse()	Reverses the order of elements in the list

Tuple Methods

Tuples are like lists, except they are immutable. This makes them a good choice for holding serial data that should not be updated. However, given that this is rarely true and that tuples are inflexible, I use them sparsely.

```
py_tuple = (8, 4, 6, 7, 3, 2, 1, 1)

print(py_tuple.count(1))
print(py_tuple.index(3))
```

Output: 2
4

Tuples have only two methods.

List Method	Definition
count()	Returns the count of a specified element in the tuple
index()	Returns the index of a specified item's 1st match from the list

MORE DETAILS ON UNORDERED COLLECTIONS

Dictionary Methods

Dictionaries are your friends when dealing with one-to-many (and sometimes many-to-many) relationships. You will often find yourselves dealing with data which is categorically grouped. I have used dictionaries in the past to store data such as:

- Vendor data, grouped by vendor name
- MACRS depreciation rates, grouped by recovery period
- Area coordinates of invoices I needed to parse using OCR
- Balance sheet data

Since dictionaries are unordered, you cannot access data through positional indexing. Instead, you can use keys to access their respective values through either the *get()* method or square brackets (more common). Another important point to note is that when you loop over a dictionary, you only loop over its keys.

```
emp_dict = {"name":"james joe", "age":35, "salary":50000}

print(emp_dict["name"].title())                    # String method
print("Annual Bonus:", emp_dict.get("salary") * .10)

emp_dict["is_retired"] = False                     # Add a new item
print(emp_dict)
```

Output: James Joe
Annual Bonus: 5000.0
{'name': 'james joe', 'age': 35, 'salary': 50000, 'is_retired': False}

```
# Consider dictionary with manufacturing overhead and related cost drivers
abc_dct = {"design":"design hours", "assembly":"# of assemblers",
                    "orders":"# of orders"}
keys = []
values = []
items = []
for act in abc_dct:
        keys.append(act)                           # Create a key list
        values.append(abc_dct[act])                # Create a value list
```

```
        items.append((act, abc_dct[act]))        # Create an item list
print("Keys -", keys)
print("Values -", values)
print("Items -", items)
```

Output: Keys - ['design', 'assembly', 'orders']
Values - ['design hours', '# of assemblers', '# of orders']
Items - [('design', 'design hours'), ('assembly', '# of assemblers'), ('orders', '# of orders')]

Dictionary keys must be of an immutable data type. To map many-to-many relationships, you can use tuples as keys for the dictionary. The three iterables created in the example above can be handily generated with the *keys()*, *values()*, and *items()* methods.

```
abc_dct = {"design":"design hours", "assembly":"# of assemblers",
                        "orders":"# of orders"}
print(abc_dct.keys())
print(abc_dct.values())
print(abc_dct.items())
```

Output: dict_keys(['design', 'assembly', 'orders'])
dict_values(['design hours', '# of assemblers', '# of orders'])
dict_items([('design', 'design hours'), ('assembly', '# of assemblers'), ('orders', '# of orders')])

Here are some dictionary methods I frequently use.

Dictionary Method	Definition
keys()	Returns an iterable containing the dictionary's keys
values()	Returns an iterable containing the dictionary's values
items()	Returns an iterable containing the dictionary's items as (key, value)
get()	Returns the corresponding value for a specified key. If a key does not exist, returns 'None'
popitem()	Removes and returns the last added item as (key, value)

Set Methods

Sets are unordered, deduplicated, and mutable. However, they can only contain immutable data types (e.g., you cannot pass a set containing a list).

Several set operations are based on the universal mathematical set theory which includes concepts such as union, intersection, and difference. These concepts are defined as set methods in Python.

1. Union

A union combines all unique elements from each set in a new set. Unions can be performed using a pipe (|) or the *union()* method.

```
X = {1, 3, 5, 7, 9}
Y = {3, 6, 9, 12, 15}

print (X|Y)
print(X.union(Y))
print(Y.union(X))
```

Output: {1, 3, 5, 6, 7, 9, 12, 15}
{1, 3, 5, 6, 7, 9, 12, 15}
{1, 3, 5, 6, 7, 9, 12, 15}

2. Intersection

An intersection returns common elements across all sets in a new set. Intersections can be performed using an ampersand (&) or the *intersection()* method.

```
X = {1, 3, 5, 7, 9}
Y = {3, 6, 9, 12, 15}

print(X & Y)
print(X.intersection(Y))
print(Y.intersection(X))
```

Output: {9, 3}
{9, 3}
{9, 3}

3. Difference

A difference returns a new set that includes values present in one set but not the other. Note that X - Y ≠ Y - X. Differences can be taken using a minus (-) or the *difference()* method.

```
X = {1, 3, 5, 7, 9}
Y = {3, 6, 9, 12, 15}

print(X - Y)
print(Y - X)
print(X.union(X - Y) == X)
print(Y.union(Y - X) == Y)
```

Output: {1, 5, 7}
{12, 6, 15}
True
True

I use sets mostly to deduplicate data. Although a mutable object cannot be a set element, a mutable iterable (such as a list) can be converted in its entirety to a set.

```
mylist = [1, 1, 2, 3, 4, 5, 5, "hello"]
set(mylist)        # Deduplicated
```

Output: {1, 2, 3, 4, 5, "hello"}

Below are some set methods.

Set Method	Definition
add()	Adds a specified element to the set
remove()	Removes a specified element from the set
pop()	Removes and returns a random element from the set
union()	Returns the union of specified sets as a new set
intersection()	Returns the intersection of specified sets as a new set
difference()	Returns the difference of specified sets as a new set
issubset()	Returns True if another specified set contains the set
issuperset()	Returns True if the set contains a specified set

DATE AND TIME

At some point, you are going to work with date and time. As a business professional (or even a programmer), working with temporal data can often be challenging. While we usually strive for regularity, dates and time are often irregular due to geographical, political, cultural, and historical differences.

Python offers three built-in modules for working with date and time:

1. **calendar**
Gregorian calendar-based methods

2. **datetime**
All classes to manipulate date and time

3. **time**
Only time methods without the date

It is likely that you will work with all three modules to get full benefit of Python's temporal capabilities.

Ticks

Computers count time starting from 00:00:00 UTC on January 1, 1970. This instance in time is known as the "Unix epoch" and is calculated at longitude 0°. UTC is appealing because it follows a consistent 24-hour day all year round without any daylight savings or other time irregularities.

Ticks refer to Python's calculation of time since the Unix epoch, in seconds.

```
import time

ticks = time.time()        # Returns ticks as of the current moment
print("Ticks since Unix epoch: ", ticks)
```

Output: Ticks since Unix epoch: 7635498.5268

It is easy to perform various time conversions, representations, and arithmetic operations using ticks. Note the limitation that ticks can only be calculated from the Unix epoch (not before) and can go up until 2038.

timetuple

Certain time methods, including *timetuple()*, return a *struct_time* object. *struct_time* is a named tuple containing stored attributes for both date and time fields. These attributes can be retrieved using their index number or attribute name.

Index	Attribute Name	Meaning	Range
0	tm_year	Year (4 digits)	e.g., 2022
1	tm_mon	Month	1 - 12
2	tm_mday	Day	1 - 31
3	tm_hour	Hour	0 - 23
4	tm_min	Minute	0 - 59
5	tm_sec	Second	0 - 61
6	tm_wday	Day of Week	0 - 6
7	tm_yday	Day of Year	1 - 366
8	tm_isdst	Daylight Saving Time	-1, 0, 1

Note that seconds go up to 61 to account for leap seconds whereas *tm_yday* goes up to 366 to account for leap years. In addition, *tm_isdst* for Daylight Saving Time shows 0 when DST is not in place, 1 when it is active, and -1 when determined by a compiler (underlying program).

```
from datetime import datetime

user_inp = str(input("Enter date in MMDDYYYY format: "))
test_date = datetime(int(user_inp[4:]), int(user_inp[:2]),
int(user_inp[2:4]))
test_date_tuple = test_date.timetuple()   # Creates a struct_time object

if test_date_tuple[0] == 2021:            # Can also access with .tm_year
        if (test_date_tuple.tm_mon - 1)//3 == 0:
                print("Date is in Q1 2021")
        elif (test_date_tuple.tm_mon - 1)//3 == 1:
                print("Date is in Q2 2021")
        elif (test_date_tuple.tm_mon - 1)//3 == 2:
                print("Date is in Q3 2021")
        elif (test_date_tuple.tm_mon - 1)//3 == 3:
```

```
            print("Date is in Q4 2021")
        else:
            print("There are only 12 months!")
else:
    print("This code is only for 2021")
```

Output: Enter date in MMDDYYYY format: 07152021

Date is in Q3 2021

timedelta

The *timedelta()* method is used to perform arithmetic operations on datetime objects. Most standard operations are supported.

```
from datetime import datetime, timedelta

test_date = datetime(2021, 12, 29)
print(test_date + timedelta(days = 2))
```

Output: 2021-12-31 00:00:00

Get Current Time

The *time()* method returns the number of ticks since the Unix epoch. You can also use the *localtime()* method to get a *struct_time* object representing the current time.

```
import time

curr_time = time.localtime()
print(time.time())
print(curr_time.tm_year, curr_time.tm_mon, curr_time.tm_mday)
```

Output: 1641797694.583371
2022 1 10

Alternatively, you can use the datetime module's *now()* method to obtain the current time as a *datetime* object:

```
from datetime import datetime

```

```
curr_time = datetime.now()
print(curr_time.year, curr_time.month, curr_time.day)
```

Output: 2022 1 10

To get the current time for a specific time zone, you can use the *pytz* module.

```
from datetime import datetime
import pytz

NYzone = pytz.timezone("America/New_York")
NYtime = datetime.now(NYzone)
print("NY time:", NYtime.strftime("%H:%M:%S"))
                                        # Formats time as needed

Londonzone = pytz.timezone("Europe/London")
Londontime = datetime.now(Londonzone)
print("London time:", Londontime.strftime("%H:%M:%S"))
```

Output: NY time: 03:45:16
London time: 08:45:16

Get Current Date

The current local date can be obtained using *date.today()* method.

```
from datetime import date

cd = date.today()
print("Today's date:", cd)
```

Output: Today's date: 2022-01-07

The above method returns a *date* object. You can change the format of the date using *strftime()*, which returns a string.

```
from datetime import date

cd = date.today()

# dd/mm/YY
print(cd.strftime("%d/%m/%Y"))
```

```
# Textual month, day and year
print(cd.strftime("%B %d, %Y"))

# mm/dd/y
print(cd.strftime("%m/%d/%y"))

# Month abbreviation, day and year
print(cd.strftime("%b-%d-%Y"))
```

Output: 10/01/2022
January 10, 2022
01/10/22
Jan-10-2022

Create a Calendar

You might need to display a calendar for any given month. You can use the *month()* method within the *calendar* module to print a specific month's calendar.

```
import calendar

yr = 2022        # year
mon = 1          # month

print(calendar.month(yr, mon))
```

Output:

```
    January 2022
Mo Tu We Th Fr Sa Su
                1  2
 3  4  5  6  7  8  9
10 11 12 13 14 15 16
17 18 19 20 21 22 23
24 25 26 27 28 29 30
31
```

MISCELLANEOUS

Following are some miscellaneous concepts I feel you should understand. Some are fundamental, while others are just efficient ways of coding that I've discovered overtime.

Importing Modules

As task complexity increases, searching for and importing appropriate modules becomes a necessity. You can access Python's built-in modules, create your own modules, and you can also download modules created by others. Remember, complex modules are often organized as packages, but the import process remains the same.

To create a module, define your required functions and then save the file with an appropriate name.

```
def add (x, y):
        result = x + y
        return result
```

Assume the file is saved as "temp_module.py."

```
import temp_module.py
temp_module.add(20, 10)
```

Output: 30

You can also import modules under an alias.

```
import mymodule as my
```

If you want to import specific modules from a package, you can do so using the *from* statement. You can import multiple modules with a single line of code.

```
# Assume inventory package with two underlying modules
from inventory import fifo, lifo

print(fifo.cogs(transaction_data))
print(lifo.cogs(transaction_data))
```

Comprehensions

Comprehensions are used to create sequences from other sequences using clear and short code. If you want to copy over a sequence but with some transformations, comprehensions can be extremely powerful; they have become one of my programming staples. Comprehensions use a *for* loop within the sequence constructor as opposed to writing the loop traditionally. There are four types of comprehension in Python.

Comprehensions are generally faster compared to traditional loops. They do not, however, possess the same versatility as loops and are thus not a replacement. Advanced iterations will still require traditional loops.

```
# Syntax
# container() denotes either [] or {}

# No condition
new_iterable = container(<expression> for <item> in
<existing_iterable>)

# if
new_iterable = container(<expression> for <item> in
<existing_iterable> if <condition>)

# if else
new_iterable = container(<expression1> if <condition> else
<expression2> for <item> in <existing_iterable>)
```

1. List Comprehension

Since you will likely use lists the most, you will likely also use list comprehensions the most. Consider the US Social Security tax. For 2022, the tax is applicable at 6.2% on earned income up to $147,000.

```
def calc_ss22(comp):
        ss = .062 * min(147000, comp)          # Returns minimum
value
        return round(ss, 2)

salaries = [15252, 18564, 50487, 102482, 150000, 205045, 93000,
147000]
```

```
# Conventional loop
ss_list1 = []
for sal in salaries:
        ss = calc_ss22(sal)
        ss_list1.append(ss)

# List comprehension
ss_list2 = [calc_ss22(sal) for sal in salaries]

print(ss_list1, "\n", ss_list2)
```

Output: [945.62, 1150.97, 3130.19, 6353.88, 9114.0, 9114.0, 5766.0, 9114.0]
[945.62, 1150.97, 3130.19, 6353.88, 9114.0, 9114.0, 5766.0, 9114.0]

Both methods yield the same output, but the list comprehension is shorter, cleaner, and faster. Notice that the tax is $9,114 for any salary over $147,000.

2. Dictionary Comprehension

You can use comprehensions to create dictionaries. However, keep in mind that dictionary comprehensions are often slower than conventional loops. In addition, all characteristics of a dictionary apply (e.g., keys should be unique and immutable).

Assume that a company's employees get a 15% bonus on their salary if their performance score is a 7 or above on a 1 – 10 scale.

```
# Dictionary formatted as {employee_name:[salary, performance_score]}
emp_details = {"a":[70000, 8], "b":[59520, 6], "c":[145000, 9],
"d":[125000, 7]}

bonus_dict = {emp:(stats + [.15 * stats[0]] if stats[1] >= 7 else stats +
[0]) for (emp, stats) in emp_details.items()}

print(bonus_dict)
```

Output: {'a': [70000, 8, 10500.0], 'b': [59520, 6, 0], 'c': [145000, 9, 21750.0], 'd': [125000, 7, 18750.0]}

3. Set Comprehension

Set comprehensions are very useful for conditionally selecting items and then deduplicating.

```
my_list = [1, 1, 2, 2, 3, 4, 6, 8, 5, 6, 7, 8, 9, 10, 11, 12, 3, 13, 15, 16, 16]

my_set = {number +2 for number in my_list if number % 2 == 0}
print (my_set)
```

Output: {4, 6, 8, 10, 12, 14, 18}

4. Generator Comprehension

There are no tuple comprehensions in Python. Instead, use of parentheses creates generator comprehensions. Create generator comprehensions if you only want something to loop over (not display, etc.). Elements within generator comprehensions cannot be accessed unless looped over. They are faster and more space efficient than any of the other comprehensions. Python functions *zip()* and *enumerate()* return generator objects, for example.

```
my_list = [1, 2, 3, 4, 5, 6, 7, 8, 9]

gen_comp = (number +2 for number in my_list if number % 2 == 0)
print(gen_comp)        # Only prints the object type and location

for number in gen_comp:
        print (number)
```

Output: <generator object <genexpr> at {some location}>

4

6

8

10

Strings that Contain Quotes

If you ever work with strings that already contain quotes, remember that Python doesn't allow a string's container to be the same as the quotes within the string. You must use double quotes ("") for strings that contain single quotes (''), and vice versa. If a string contains both double and single quotes, use triple quotes ("""""").

```
print("Python for accounting is "smooth" to learn!")
```

Output: SyntaxError: invalid syntax

```
print('Python for accounting is "smooth" to learn!')
```

Output: Python for accounting is "smooth" to learn!

```
print("""He said, "the LIFO reserve's calculation is what's confusing,"
and I agreed""")
```

Output: He said, "the LIFO reserve's calculation is what's confusing," and I agreed

Select Iterables

There are certain built-in iterable types in Python that are very similar to (but not the same as) generator comprehensions. These can be of good use if you want to loop over two or more sequences simultaneously.

1. range

The built-in *range()* function is used to generate a sequence of numbers for a specified range. You can use it to loop a specific number of times over any iterable.

```
# Syntax
range(stop)                    # Defaults to start = 0 and step = 1
# or
range(start, stop, step)       # Inclusive of start, exclusive of stop
```

```
# Calling only the stop argument
# 'i' denotes one element
# In loops, any name may be used to denote a single element
mylist = []
for i in range(8):
	mylist.append(i)
print(mylist)
```

Output: [0, 1, 2, 3, 4, 5, 6, 7]

```
mylist = []
for num in range(3, 8):
	mylist.append(num)
print(mylist)
```

Output: [3, 4, 5, 6, 7]

```
mylist = []
for any_name in range(2, 20, 2):
	mylist.append(any_name)
print(mylist)
```

Output: [2, 4, 6, 8, 10, 12, 14, 16, 18]

```
# Range in descending order (reversed) using negative step value
mylist = []
for i in range(18, 0, -2):
        mylist.append(i)
print(mylist)
```

Output: [18, 16, 14, 12, 10, 8, 6, 4, 2]

```
# Accessing range items using indices
x = range(8)[2]
y = range(8) [-2]

print ("x =", x)
print ("y =", y)
```

Output: x = 2
y = 6

2. zip

The *zip()* function maps two or more iterables together, such that you can loop over all simultaneously. All iterables must be of the same length. Items are mapped in the order they appear, which is why you should only use sequences within this function. Using collections will result in unexpected results because they are unordered.

```
# Syntax
zip(iterators)
```

For me, two of the most common uses for the *zip* function are looping over multiple columns in an Excel file together (for example, search an invoice using one column, download it, and rename it using the other column) and creating a dictionary to map multiple iterables.

```
# Zipping two lists
employee = ["Emma", "Amy", "John", "Adam"]
id = [45214, 879452, "45AW3", "4B32C"]

mapped = {i:j for i, j in zip(employee, id)}
print(mapped)
```

Output: {'Emma': 45214, 'Amy': 879452, 'John': '45AW3', 'Adam': '4B32C'}

3. enumerate

The *enumerate()* function is a variation of *zip()* where the first iterable is *range()*. It is used to add a "counter" to your sequence. It takes a single iterable as argument.

```
# Syntax
enumerate(iterable, start)   # Defaults to start = 0
                             # Equivalent to zip(range(len(iterable),
iterable)
```

```
vendors = ["a pharama", "b motors", "c consulting", "d farms"]

add_counter_0 = enumerate(vendors)
add_counter_3 = enumerate(vendors, 3)

print(type(add_counter_0))
print(list(add_counter_0))
print(list(add_counter_3))
```

Output: <class 'enumerate'>
[(0, 'a pharama'), (1, 'b motors'), (2, 'c consulting'), (3, 'd farms')]
[(3, 'a pharama'), (4, 'b motors'), (5, 'c consulting'), (6, 'd farms')]

any, all

Often, you will encounter situations where you must determine if one or more relationships in your data exist. An action may be executed only when some or all instances of a particular condition are met. For example, an adjusting entry upload would happen only if all proposed entries have been reviewed by the audit client. Your depreciation schedule may not require a salvage value when using any form of declining balance method. Or your bot may not execute some code unless any/all of some conditions are met.

Both *any()* and *all()* are used to see if items in an iterable are True or False. Both functions are not very useful unless exposed to some "truth" test. Sounds technical, but it is fairly straightforward.

In Python, almost anything can technically evaluate to True/False. The integer 1 will evaluate to True, because it is "Truthy" (weird sounding phrase, but I interpret it as "feels" true). Contrarily, 0 evaluates to False because it is "Falsy," as do empty sequences. Virtually everything else evaluates to True.

```
mylist = [1, "a", "hello", 0, ()]
for item in mylist:
        print(item, ":", bool(item))
```

Output: 1 : True
a : True
hello : True
0 : False
() : False

This is not as useful as, say, the below.

```
mylist = [1, "a", "hello", 0, ()]
for item in mylist:
        print(item, "is integer:", type(item) == int)
```

Output: 1 is integer: True
a is integer: False
hello is integer: False

0 is integer: True
() is integer: False

Note that the *bool()* function is not required here because the comparison operator (==) calls it implicitly. A quick way to remember this: an expression that automatically evaluates to a Boolean value, as opposed to after *bool()* being explicitly called, likely has a clearer purpose and more information value.

```
# Syntax
any(iterable)
all(iterable)
```

The *any()* function returns True if any item of the iterable evaluates to True. The *all()* function returns True if all items of the iterable evaluate to True. Both functions return False otherwise.

Remember, *any()* and *all()* readily apply a truth test to the items of an iterable, without any modifications or transformations. This means that whatever condition you want to test must already have been applied to the iterable's items before passing them through the function. I stress this because it took me a while to understand the mechanism.

```
# Assume "asset_type" is a list containing all asset types of a company

test_list = ["cash", "PPE", "inventory", "software", "loans lent",
"goodwill"]

# Returns True but is not useful. Just checks the truthiness of the items
# Checks if any of the items are not 0, "", [], (), False
any(test_list)

# Returns False for technical reasons I will not delve into
# NOT correct. Condition must be evaluated within the iterable, not
outside
any(test_list) in asset_type

# Correct. Condition is within the iterable, using list comprehension
# Assume the company has cash as its only asset
# The resultant list is [True, False, False, False, False, False]
```

```
any([(asset in asset_type) for asset in test_list])

test_result1 = any([(asset in asset_type) for asset in test_list])
test_result2 = all([(asset in asset_type) for asset in test_list])

print("Are any of these the company's assets?", test_result1)
print("Are all these the company's assets? ", test_result2)
```

Output: Are any of these the company's assets? True
Are all of these the company's assets? False

Both *any()* and *all()* are powerful functions but require a strong understanding of Python mechanisms to be executed correctly. This becomes especially true as your programs (and consequently conditions) get more complex.

len

You can use the *len()* function in Python to obtain the total count of elements, or "length," of a data type. The object must be a sequence or some type of collection.

```
len(object)      # Must be an iterable
```

If called upon a data type that has no length, the function will throw an error.

```
my_list = ["a", "b", "c", "d", "e", "f"]
print ("Length of list:", len(my_list))

my_string = "abcdef"
print(len(my_list) == len(my_string))

print(len(5))
```

Output: Length of list: 6
True
TypeError: object of type 'int' has no len()

f-strings

f-strings are used to add values to placeholders in a string. They can dynamically replace parts of a string. You can do this by adding the prefix "f" to a string and including the dynamic parts in curly brackets ({}). There are other ways to dynamically update strings, but f-string formatting is the latest and most flexible innovation.

f-strings are extremely powerful and very important! I have used them in many automations I have created. A few uses of f-strings follow:

- Dynamically assign names to downloaded files.
- Dynamically update temporal code with different dates.
- Create written memos for multiple purposes by dynamically replacing keywords.
- Anytime you want to create multiple copies of the same item with a few modifications for each copy.
- Dynamically execute Python code! This is possible in conjunction with the *exec* function, but is also risky.

```
x = 'Python'
y = 'Accounting & Business'
print(f"This book is titled {x} for {y}")

name = 'John'
role = 'CPA'
company = 'ABC Corporation'
print(f"{name} is a {role} at {company}")

import datetime
today = datetime.datetime.today()
print(f"{today: %B %d, %Y}")          # Embedding function result
```

Output: This book is titled Python for Accounting & Business
John is a CPA at ABC Corporation
January 12, 2022

Consider a private equity fund that pays an annual 8% simple interest. The fund is sending out an informational memo to its investors. Since partner details remain unchanged except for a one-time yearly update, the fund stores this data in tuples. Note the character combination (:,) which can be used to format a "numeric" string with commas.

```
# Dictionary formatted as {prtnr_name:(init_invest, num_yrs)}
prtnr_dtls = {"John Pythonista":(186754, 5), "Crimson Tuple":(347176, 1), "Leslie Float":(412200, 3), "Desiree Loop":(231400, 1), "Antonio Coder":(114715, 2)}

for name, det in prtnr_dtls.items():

        memo = f"""Dear {name.split()[0]},
You are receiving this email because you are a partner in the fund ABC Fund, LP. As of December 31, 2021, you have a total investment of ${det[0] + (det[0] * .08 * det[1]) :,}, which includes the original principal amount of ${det[0] :,} and cumulative dividends of ${det[0] * .08 * det[1] :,} over your {det[1]} year(s) in the fund.
Thank you,
Management"""

        print(memo, "\n")
```

Output:
Dear John,
You are receiving this email because you are a partner in ABC Fund, LP. As of December 31, 2021, you have a total investment of $261,455.6, which includes the original principal amount of $186,754 and cumulative dividends of $74,701.6 over your 5 year(s) in the fund.
Thank you,
Management

Dear Crimson,
You are receiving this email because you are a partner in ABC Fund, LP. As of December 31, 2021, you have a total investment of $374,950.08, which includes the original principal amount of $347,176 and cumulative dividends of $27,774.08 over your 1 year(s) in the fund.
Thank you,
Management

Dear Leslie,
You are receiving this email because you are a partner in ABC Fund, LP. As of

December 31, 2021, you have a total investment of $511,128.0, which includes the original principal amount of $412,200 and cumulative dividends of $98,928.0 over your 3 year(s) in the fund.
Thank you,
Management

Dear Desiree,
You are receiving this email because you are a partner in ABC Fund, LP. As of December 31, 2021, you have a total investment of $249,912.0, which includes the original principal amount of $231,400 and cumulative dividends of $18,512.0 over your 1 year(s) in the fund.
Thank you,
Management

Dear Antonio,
You are receiving this email because you are a partner in ABC Fund, LP. As of December 31, 2021, you have a total investment of $133,069.4, which includes the original principal amount of $114,715 and cumulative dividends of $18,354.4 over your 2 year(s) in the fund.
Thank you,
Management

Notice how f-strings efficiently automate a task that would otherwise have taken several hours to complete (for example, if there were 10,000 investors). If you regularly work with textual data, f-strings should be on the top of the list of techniques you should master. Do refer to other, more in-depth resources to fully understand f-strings.

exec

The *exec()* function is as close as it gets to a developer-intended function in this book. I am including this function because I have used it sparingly, although I am trying to limit its use further.

This function is used to dynamically execute objects, especially strings, as Python code. You can write your code within a string, and *exec()* will run the string as a Python code! Combined with the massive manipulative capabilities of Python strings, *exec()* can produce extremely powerful, program-altering codes that can accomplish in a few lines what otherwise would taken many.

```
# Syntax
exec(object)                # Mostly strings
```

There are also optional global and local arguments that can be passed, but they are beyond the scope of this book.

```
random_math_str = "((300 + 65) * 4) % 33"
print(random_math_str, "|", type(random_math_str))
```

*Output: ((300 + 65) * 4) % 33 | <class 'str'>*

Compare the above example to the below.

```
# Put the entire line within a string; exec executes the string as code
my_str = "random_math_str = ((300 + 65) * 4) % 33"
exec(my_str)
print(random_math_str, "|", type(random_math_str))
```

Output: 8 | <class 'int'>

Note that *exec()* never returns a value. If you just pass an expression, you will get no result in return. You must assign your expression to a variable ("my_str" in the example above) to be able to access the result later.

A classic example where this function is warranted is when you have several datasets/tables that you need to assign to individual variables. Assume that you have 100 tables that you need to collectively work with. You want to assign each table to a variable. Rather than assigning manually, you can use the *exec()* function to dynamically create new variables.

```
# Assume each table is a pandas dataframe object
tables = [table1, table2, table3, ……………………..., table100]

# Use exec() with f-string
for num, table in enumerate(tables, start = 1):
        exec(f"a{num} = tables[{num - 1}]")
```

The above code creates 100 variables (a1, a2, a3, ……, a100) and assigns a dataframe to each. This is significantly more efficient than manually creating these variables.

Always use *exec()* as a last resort! Dynamic code execution creates the potential for many vulnerabilities within your code. For example, anyone who uses your code may be able to alter it using this function. Never include *exec()* within an *input* statement. This function is generally intended for advanced developers who create back-end applications.

The sheer power of this function makes it "addictive." If you must use it, I highly recommend you contain *exec()* by limiting the code passed through it. Only use *exec()* when it is absolutely necessary to improve the overall performance of your code and to automate complex tasks.

SECTION 03
HANDS-ON

CHAPTER 06 | **PYTHON LIBRARIES FOR BUSINESS**

After you have a grasp on the foundational framework of Python, you should explore specialized libraries. Some of these libraries are of such importance that they could be categorized as a "de-facto" part of the foundational framework. Others are narrower in scope and are used for specialized purposes. Regardless, remember that Python libraries are, at the end of the day, a collection of Python code. They are based on foundational concepts. If you are fluent with these concepts, you should have little trouble learning new libraries.

The term "library" has not been defined in the official Python documentation. The documentation does, however, refer to Python's standard/built-in collection of code as the Python Standard Library. I think of a library as any collection of codes developed for a specific purpose. A library may be a module, package, or anything between the two.

In this chapter, I go over select libraries that I have used and that I believe can be applicable for accounting and/or business-related work. These libraries offer functionalities that will help you in automating tasks and creating bespoke accounting tools and software for individual situations. Note that many of the libraries are very broad, and I will as such go over the salient features. When I provide the syntax of a particular method, it is quite possible that it will not be all-inclusive. Some of the syntaxes can be very long; I only provide arguments that are likely to be repeatedly used.

Also note that I only go over what I consider to be "foundational" libraries that I use in a business setting. For more advanced libraries, stay tuned for my upcoming Volume 2 of this book!

THE ESSENTIALS

PANDAS

pandas is a *very* important toolkit at your disposal, perhaps second only to the core Python concepts. It'll form the basis of your business/accounting data analysis in Python. Although it is not a standard package, it may as well be. You will import pandas in virtually any code you write, because it is usually the default library for parsing and storing spreadsheet data.

pandas is a data analysis library that supports heterogeneous data types and allows you to store and manipulate data in tabular format. It is a vast library that has been in constant development, with periodic updates since 2008 when it was first created by Wes McKinney. At its core, pandas is a data analysis library. However, what sets it apart is its structured approach towards data storage, organization, and manipulation (precisely what sets Excel apart). This translates into several advantages:

1. Data manipulation is effective and (cautiously) fast.
2. Heterogeneous data types can be stored within the same structure.
3. Missing data can be efficiently managed.
4. Multiple datasets can be easily and quickly merged or joined.
5. Split-apply-combine operations on datasets can be performed through effective group-by functionality.
6. Datasets can be flexibly reshaped and pivoted.

pandas is easy (but extensive) to learn and use, and can be modified to meet your particular programming needs. There are several libraries that depend on pandas. Many of these libraries fall within the domain of automation and data science. For example, Matplotlib uses pandas for plotting functions, SciPy for statistical analysis, scikit-learn for machine learning, FFN for financial analysis, etc.

The first step is always to import the relevant library. For all following pandas examples going forward, assume that the library has been imported.

```
# Any alias may be provided, but pd is conventional
import pandas as pd
```

Data Structures in pandas

There are two main types of data structures in pandas: Series and DataFrame.

1. Series

Series are one-dimensional labeled data structures used to store any type of data. They are analogous to columns in Microsoft Excel. You can create series from any *ordered* data structure, such as a sequence. An exception to this rule is that series can be created from a dictionary.

```
data = ['p', 'y', 't', 'h', 'o', 'n']
ser = pd.Series(data)

print(type(ser))
print(ser)
```

Output: <class 'pandas.core.series.Series'>

```
0   p
1   y
2   t
3   h
4   o
5   n
dtype: object
```

A pandas series will always be accompanied by an index, just like a list or a tuple. However, a series will explicitly print its index when called. You can also update a series' index as you see fit.

```
tax_yr = ['2015', '2016', '2017']      # Better as text. No numerical utility
tax_amt = [200.65, 754.14, 300.58]

ser = pd.Series(tax_amt, index = tax_yr)

print(ser)
print("\n", "Total Taxes = $", sum(ser))        # sum is native Python
```

Output:

```
2015    200.65
2016    754.14
```

2017   300.58
dtype: float64

Total Taxes = $ 1255.37

While pandas series have some utility, they are not used much in practice. Uni-dimensional data rarely needs to be stored as a series. Another (simpler) data structure such as a list is usually more appropriate. The real power of pandas is evident when dealing with bi-dimensional data.

2. DataFrame

DataFrame is a two-dimensional (rows and columns) labeled data structure. It is a combination of multiple pandas series, all of which are joined over a common index.

A dataframe functions much like a spreadsheet and is the primary pandas data structure. They are also arguably the most used data type for storing tabular data in Python. Several other libraries conduct their I/O operations through pandas dataframes. Because business data is overwhelmingly stored in tabular format (.xlsx, .csv, or .txt), dataframe is your "staple" type to import any kind of data in Python.

Although not usually needed, there are ways to format dataframes to display more than two dimensions.

Creating a pandas DataFrame

There are four "native" ways to create a dataframe in pandas. Many other function-based ways exist.

Method 1: Lists of lists/tuples

Store multiple lists/tuples within a list. Dataframe columns are created by grouping values by index positions. Column names must be explicitly passed or will default to a 0-indexed range. I prefer to pass column names using an immutable data type, although this is not necessary.

```
data = [['John', 24, 4000], ['Elise', 23, 4500], ['Amy', 27, 3000]]
df = pd.DataFrame(data, columns = ("Name", "Age", " Pay"))
df
```

Output:

	Name	Age	Pay
0	John	24	4000
1	Elise	23	4500
2	Amy	27	3000

Method 2: Dictionary of lists

Create a dictionary that maps column names to list of values.

```
data = {'Name': ['David', 'Joyce', 'Lisa', 'Rackham'], 'Age': [33, 45, 26, 
58]}
df = pd.DataFrame(data)        # DataFrame is case-sensitive
df
```

Output:

	Name	Age
0	David	33
1	Joyce	45
2	Lisa	26
3	Rackham	58

Method 3: List of dictionaries

Create a list of dictionaries. Each dictionary maps column names to corresponding values.

```
data = [{'AcctNo' : '12451', 'AcctName': 'Cash on Hand', 'AcctBal' : 
56452},
        {'AcctNo' : '22652', 'AcctName': 'Land', 'AcctBal' : 356420}]

accts = pd.DataFrame(data)
accts
```

Output:

	AcctNo	AcctName	AcctBal
0	12451	Cash on Hand	56452
1	22652	Land	356420

A custom index must be explicitly passed for methods 1, 2, and 3. Otherwise, they default to a 0-indexed range. In practice, having custom column names is much more common than a custom index (how often do you name your rows in Excel?).

```
# Method 2
data = {'Name':['David', 'Joyce', 'Lisa', 'Rackham'], 'Salary':[60, 80, 95,
120]}
df = pd.DataFrame(data, index = ['associate', 'senior', 'manager',
'partner'])
df
```

Output:

	Name	*Salary*
associate	*David*	*60*
senior	*Joyce*	*80*
manager	*Lisa*	*95*
partner	*Rack*	*120*

Method 4: Dictionary of dictionaries

This is the only method that allows for specifying a custom index within the formation. Create a dictionary that maps each column to another dictionary of index-value pairs. A custom index need not be explicitly passed.

```
data = {'Name':{'associate':'David', 'senior':'Joyce', 'manager':'Lisa',
'partner':'Rack'}, 'Salary':{'associate':60, 'senior':80, 'manager':95,
'partner':120}}

df = pd.DataFrame(data)
df
```

Output:

	Name	*Salary*
associate	*David*	*60*
senior	*Joyce*	*80*
manager	*Lisa*	*95*
partner	*Rack*	*120*

Adding/Removing Columns

There are several ways to add/delete a column to/from an existing DataFrame. Adding rows is not as straightforward since it requires a manipulation across series. It is not complicated either, though, and will be covered later.

The two most used ways for inserting a new column are as follows:

Method 1: Direct Assignment

One of the most common ways is to directly assign a sequence to a new column within the dataframe. This method does not issue an explicit function call, but is only applicable to adding columns (not to adding rows or deleting columns/rows). It always adds the new column to the far right.

Since dataframes are a collection of multiple series (as columns), you can access each series by an explicit call to the column name (much like accessing a value within a dictionary by calling the corresponding key). Below I start creating a fixed asset schedule. I carry this dataframe over for other examples.

```
# Fixed asset schedule. F&F is Furniture & Fixtures
fa = pd.DataFrame({"Category":["Land", "Building", "Equipment",
"Equipment", "Appliance", "F&F", "Building"]})

fa["Price"] = [300000, 150000, 200000, 45000, 3500, 7500, 350000]
fa
```

Output:

	Category	Price
0	Land	300000
1	Building	150000
2	Equipment	200000
3	Equipment	45000
4	Appliance	3500
5	F&F	7500
6	Building	350000

Individual columns in the dataframe may also be accessed in a similar way.

```
# Single square brackets
```

```
fa["Category"]          # Returns a pandas series. Equivalent to
fa.Category
```

Output: *0 Land*
1 Building
2 Equipment
3 Equipment
4 Appliance
5 F&F
6 Building
Name: Category, dtype: object

```
# Double square brackets
fa[["Category"]]        # Returns a pandas dataframe
                        # Notice the column name on top of the output
```

Output: *Category*
0 Land
1 Building
2 Equipment
3 Equipment
4 Appliance
5 F&F
6 Building

Method 2: df.insert()

This method is useful if you want to insert a column at a specific location, not necessarily at the end.

```
# Syntax
df.insert(location, column_name, iterable)      # df denotes dataframe
```

```
names_tuple = ("Plot", "Office", "Roller", "Forklift", "Furnace",
"Windows", "Factory")                            # Using lists is not a
necessity

fa.insert(1, "Name", names_tuple)      # location is 0-indexed
fa
```

Output:

	Category	*Name*	*Price*
0	*Land*	*Plot*	*300000*
1	*Building*	*Office*	*150000*
2	*Equipment*	*Roller*	*200000*
3	*Equipment*	*Forklift*	*45000*
4	*Appliance*	*Furnace*	*3500*
5	*F&F*	*Windows*	*7500*
6	*Building*	*Factory*	*350000*

You can delete a column in one of three ways.

Method 1: del

The *del* function is not specific to pandas; it is a Python function used to delete objects from memory. You can use *del* to delete dataframe columns, one at a time.

```
del fa["Name"]
fa
```

Output:

	Category	*Price*
0	*Land*	*300000*
1	*Building*	*150000*
2	*Equipment*	*200000*
3	*Equipment*	*45000*
4	*Appliance*	*3500*
5	*F&F*	*7500*
6	*Building*	*350000*

Method 2: df.drop()

The *drop()* method lets you drop multiple columns <u>or rows</u> simultaneously.

```
# Syntax
# Specify either index or column. <d> denotes default value
df.drop(OR<index, columns> = labels_to_drop, inplace = False <d>)
```

For many dataframe methods, the optional argument *inplace* can be specified. If set to False (default), the underlying operation is performed but the existing dataframe object is <u>not</u> updated. The result is returned as a new dataframe which can then be assigned to a variable. Contrarily, if set to True, the operation is performed "in-place" and the existing object is updated; nothing is returned.

```
fa.insert(1, "Name", names_tuple)       # Adding back the deleted
column

fa1 = fa.drop(columns = ['Name', 'Price'])      # inplace = False
print("fa1:\n", fa1, "\n\nfa:\n", fa)     # Original frame unchanged
```

Output: fa1:

	Category
0	*Land*
1	*Building*
2	*Equipment*
3	*Equipment*
4	*Appliance*
5	*F&F*
6	*Building*

fa:

	Category	*Name*	*Price*
0	*Land*	*Plot*	*300000*
1	*Building*	*Office*	*150000*
2	*Equipment*	*Roller*	*200000*
3	*Equipment*	*Forklift*	*45000*
4	*Appliance*	*Furnace*	*3500*
5	*F&F*	*Windows*	*7500*
6	*Building*	*Factory*	*350000*

```
fa.drop(columns = ['Name', 'Price'], inplace = True)
                                        # Need not assign to a new variable
print("fa:\n", fa)                      # Original frame updated
```

Output: fa:

	Category
0	*Land*
1	*Building*

2	*Equipment*
3	*Equipment*
4	*Appliance*
5	*F&F*
6	*Building*

Method 3: df.pop()

Note that *drop()* returns either nothing or the updated dataframe, but loses the dropped column(s). The *pop()* method deletes a column from the dataframe in-place and then returns the dropped column. This can be handy if you want to remove a column from a dataframe and hold it standalone or add it to another dataframe. You can only delete one column per *pop()* call.

```
# Syntax
df.pop(column)
```

You can only delete one column per *pop()* call.

```
fa.insert(1, "Name", names_tuple)
fa.insert(2, "Price", [300000, 150000, 200000, 45000, 3500, 7500,
350000])

cat = fa.pop('Category')                    # pop returns a pandas series
print("cat:\n", pd.DataFrame(cat), "\n\nfa:\n", fa)
```

Output: cat:

	Category
0	*Land*
1	*Building*
2	*Equipment*
3	*Equipment*
4	*Appliance*
5	*F&F*
6	*Building*

fa:

	Name	*Price*
0	*Plot*	*300000*

1	*Office*	*150000*
2	*Roller*	*200000*
3	*Forklift*	*45000*
4	*Furnace*	*3500*
5	*Windows*	*7500*
6	*Factory*	*350000*

```
fa.insert(0, "Category", ["Land", "Building", "Equipment",
"Equipment", "Appliance", "F&F", "Building"])        # Make whole
```

Filtering

There are many ways to filter data in pandas. Below are two of the most common techniques. Check out the pandas documentation for other, more targeted ways.

Method 1: Direct Filtering

Direct filtering is the most flexible and comprehensive.

```
# Syntax
df[filter_condition]
```

Assume straight-line depreciation [(Purchase Price – Salvage Value)/Useful Life] and no salvage value for each asset.

```
# Add useful life
fa["Life"] = ['Inf', 30, 5, 7, 10, 8, 15]

# Add yearly depreciation
fa['Yrly Depr'] = ['NA' if ul == 'Inf' else round(pp/ul, 2) for pp, ul in
zip(fa['Price'], fa['Life'])]        # List comprehension

fa
```

Output:	*Category*	*Name*	*Price*	*Life*	*Yrly Depr*
0	*Land*	*Plot*	*300000*	*Inf*	*NA*
1	*Building*	*Office*	*150000*	*30*	*5000.0*
2	*Equipment*	*Roller*	*200000*	*5*	*40000.0*
3	*Equipment*	*Forklift*	*45000*	*7*	*6428.57*
4	*Appliance*	*Furnace*	*3500*	*10*	*350.0*

5	*F&F*	*Windows*	*7500*	*8*	*937.5*
6	*Building*	*Factory*	*350000*	*15*	*23333.33*

Much like you can directly assign a column to a dataframe, you can directly filter data using logical operators.

```
fa[fa.Price < 100000]
```

Output:	*Category*	*Name*	*Price*	*Life*	*Yrly Depr*
3	*Equipment*	*Forklift*	*45000*	*7*	*6428.57*
4	*Appliance*	*Furnace*	*3500*	*10*	*350.0*
5	*F&F*	*Windows*	*7500*	*8*	*937.5*

As opposed to memorizing filter conditions, understanding how direct filtering works can exponentially increase its utility. Under the hood, direct filtering requires a sequence of Boolean values within square brackets. The dataframe is filtered on index/row positions that correspond to True. For example, *fa.Price < 100000* generates the series *pd.Series([False, False, False, True, True, True, False*]), one value for each row in the frame. When running *fa[fa.Price < 100000]*, the program actually executes *fa[pd.Series([False, False, False, True, True, True, False])]*. Retaining only True rows returns the filtered output above.

```
# Notice "&". Do not confuse with the Boolean "and"
# Both are similar but have subtle, technical differences

# Equivalent to fa[[False, False, False, False, False, False, True]]
fa[(fa.Category == 'Building') & (fa['Price'] > 200000)]
```

Output:	*Category*	*Name*	*Price*	*Life*	*Yrly Depr*
6	*Building*	*Factory*	*350000*	*15*	*23333.33*

Note that direct filtering can be performed using other sequence types, which broadens a dataframe's filtering potential. You can create filters externally in any way and use on a dataframe. As long as you pass a sequence of Booleans that has a length equal to the number of rows in the dataframe, your dataframe will be filtered. Assume you want to filter all assets that are either land or have a useful life of at most 10 years.

```
# Notice "|". Do not confuse with the Boolean "or"
```

```
# Both are similar but have subtle, technical differences
fa[(fa.Category == 'Land') | (fa.Life <= 10)]
```

Output: TypeError: '<=' not supported between instances of 'str' and 'int'

The above code errors out because the "Life" column contains both string and numeric data types. Comparing strings and integers with the <= operator is illegal. As a solution, you can create an external filter that defaults to True for all assets that are land and evaluates the useful life for all other assets.

```
# External filter
my_filter = [True if cat == "Land" else ul <= 10 for cat, ul in
zip(fa.Category, fa.Life)]

fa[my_filter]
```

Output:

	Category	Name	Price	Life	Yrly Depr
0	Land	Plot	300000	Inf	NA
2	Equipment	Roller	200000	5	40000.0
3	Equipment	Forklift	45000	7	6428.57
4	Appliance	Furnace	3500	10	350.0
5	F&F	Windows	7500	8	937.5

You can also use the *isin()* method to filter for data contained in a particular sequence. This is a method of both dataframes and series, although the series counterpart is generally more useful for filtering.

```
fa[(fa.Name.isin(["Plot", "Forklift", "Windows"])) & (fa.Category !=
'Land')]
```

Output:

	Category	Name	Price	Life	Yrly Depr
3	Equipment	Forklift	45000	7	6428.57
5	F&F	Windows	7500	8	937.5

When filtering textual data, you can apply most string methods using the string accessor of pandas series. These methods are found within the *str* attribute and are mostly the same as conventional string methods.

```
fa[fa.Name.str.startswith("F")]
```

Output:

	Category	Name	Price	Life	Yrly Depr
3	Equipment	Forklift	45000	7	6428.57
4	Appliance	Furnace	3500	10	350.0
6	Building	Factory	350000	15	23333.33

```
# Not a conventional string method
fa[fa.Category.str.contains("&")]                    # Substitute for "in"
operator
```

Output:

	Category	Name	Price	Life	Yrly Depr
5	F&F	Windows	7500	8	937.5

Method 2: df.filter()

pandas offers the *filter()* method to filter either axis (rows/columns) based on axis names/labels. This is useful when you want to filter not on the contents of a dataframe but on row/column names. Note that *filter()* is also available for series.

```
Syntax
# axis = 0/'index' OR 1/'columns'
df.filter(OR<labels <d>, like, regex> = criteria, axis = 1 <d>)
```

You can filter on one of three criteria: a sequence of labels that occur in the axis, a regular expression (regex) specifying the search pattern for labels, or a *like* argument which selects labels containing a specified string. For dataframes, the default criterion is *labels* and the default axis is 1 (which can also be passed as "columns").

```
fa.filter(['Name', 'Life'])                 # items = ['Name', 'Life'], axis =
1
```

Output:

	Name	Life
0	Plot	Inf
1	Office	30
2	Roller	5
3	Forklift	7
4	Furnace	10
5	Windows	8
6	Factory	15

```
fa.filter(range(5), axis = 0)          # Filter first 5 rows
```

Output:

	Category	Name	Price	Life	Yrly Depr
0	Land	Plot	300000	Inf	NA
1	Building	Office	150000	30	5000.0
2	Equipment	Roller	200000	5	40000.0
3	Equipment	Forklift	45000	7	6428.57
4	Appliance	Furnace	3500	10	350.0

```
fa.filter(like = "ri")
```

Output:

	Price
0	300000
1	150000
2	200000
3	45000
4	3500
5	7500
6	350000

```
fa.filter(range(0, 7, 2), axis = "rows")
```

Output:

	Category	Name	Price	Life	Yrly Depr
0	Land	Plot	300000	Inf	NA
2	Equipment	Roller	200000	5	40000.0
4	Appliance	Furnace	3500	10	350.0
6	Building	Factory	350000	15	23333.33

Merge, Join, and Concatenate Dataframes

Joining two tables on common data is a staple in data analysis. You can perform all types of joins on pandas dataframes. You can also concatenate, or "stack," multiple pandas dataframes.

How Joins Work

Joins are used to combine two or more datasets based on common keys, which can be columns/rows. Different types of joins return different outputs. Joins can quickly get complicated. Below I describe the four most common join operations (accompanying images taken, with written permission, from; https://datascienceparichay.com/article/understanding-joins-in-pandas).

1. Inner Join

An inner join returns only those records that are common between all joined dataframes. This is essentially an intersection of all dataframes. In

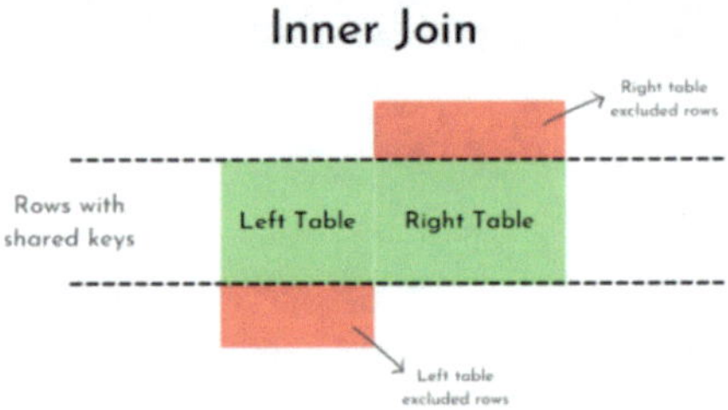

the figure below, the green represents rows included in the result of the inner join operation. The red represents excluded rows.

2. Left Join

A left join, also known as a left outer join, returns all rows from the left dataframe. The subset of rows matching with the right dataframe include new data from the right. Rows from the left that do not match to the

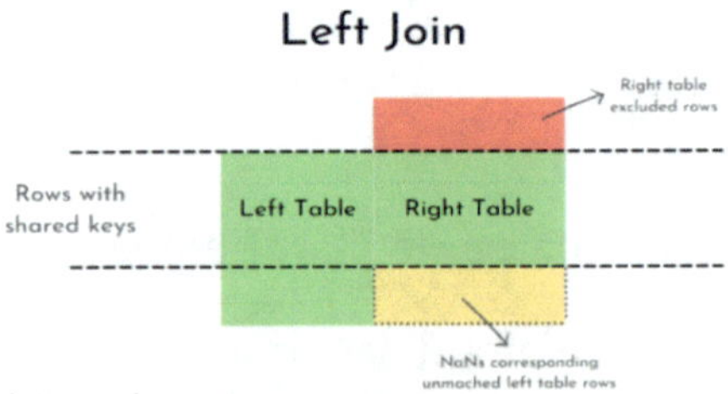

right return with nulls for the new data. In cases where the left table rows have no match in the right table, the outcome will result in Null values (NaN if applying join in pandas).

3. Right Join

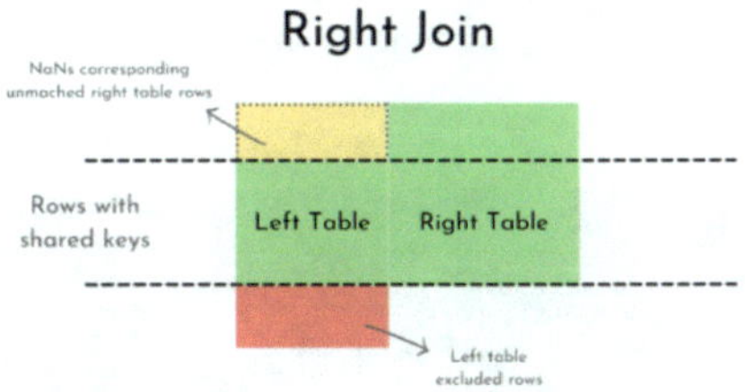

A right join is the opposite of a left join. It returns all rows from the right dataframe, with the joined rows having new data from the left and the unjoined having nulls.

4. Outer Join

A full outer join includes all rows from both left and right dataframes. Rows that fail to have a matching key in either of the two sides show null values.

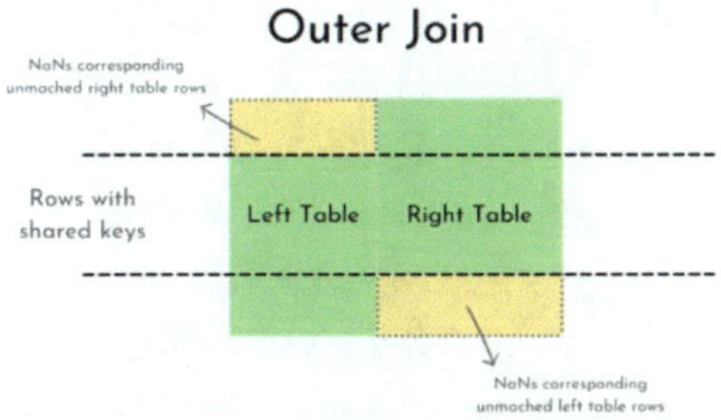

pd.concat()

The *concat()* method is straightforward: you can use it to "stack" multiple dataframes together, either vertically or horizontally. pandas automatically matches the relevant axes of all dataframes for concatenation. Note that *concat()* is a high-level library (and not a dataframe) function. This means that you call it directly from the pandas library and not from a dataframe object.

```
# Syntax
pd.concat(sequence_of_dfs, axis = 0 <d>, join = 'outer' <d>,
ignore_index = False <d>)
```

By default, *concat()* performs an outer join on rows (0/'index') and preserves the axis labels of each dataframe. Specifying *ignore_index = True* resets the concatenation axis of the resulting dataframe to a 0-indexed series.

```
fa_add = pd.DataFrame([["Land Imp", "Road", 175000, 20,
round(175000/20, 2)], ["Auto", "Car", 22000, 3, round(22000/3, 2)]],
columns = fa.columns)                    # Two new assets

fa_add
```

Output:	*Category*	*Name*	*Price*	*Life*	*Yrly Depr*
0	*Land Imp*	*Road*	*175000*	*20*	*8750.00*
1	*Auto*	*Car*	*22000*	*3*	*7333.33*

```
fa = pd.concat([fa, fa_add], ignore_index = True)
fa
```

Output:	*Category*	*Name*	*Price*	*Life*	*Yrly Depr*
0	*Land*	*Plot*	*300000*	*Inf*	*NA*
1	*Building*	*Office*	*150000*	*30*	*5000.0*
2	*Equipment*	*Roller*	*200000*	*5*	*40000.0*
3	*Equipment*	*Forklift*	*45000*	*7*	*6428.57*
4	*Appliance*	*Furnace*	*3500*	*10*	*350.0*
5	*F&F*	*Windows*	*7500*	*8*	*937.5*
6	*Building*	*Factory*	*350000*	*15*	*23333.33*
7	*Land Imp*	*Road*	*175000*	*20*	*8750.00*
8	*Auto*	*Car*	*22000*	*3*	*7333.33*

```
yrly_depr = fa.pop("Yrly Depr")              # Delete and return column
fa = pd.concat((fa, yrly_depr), axis = 1)     # Make whole

yrly_depr                                     # concat also accepts series
```

Output:	
0	*NA*
1	*5000.0*
2	*40000.0*
3	*6428.57*
4	*350.0*
5	*937.5*
6	*23333.33*

7 8750.0
8 7333.33
Name: Yrly Depr, dtype: object

df.merge()

For joins that are not a simple concatenation, you can use the *merge()* method. The pandas *merge()* is very comprehensive. Options include index-to-index, column-to-column, index-to-column, and column-to-index joins. Types of joins include left, right, inner, outer, and cross. One limitation of *merge()* is that it is limited to joining two dataframes, not any more.

For financial reporting, entities in the US are free to use their own useful lives for assets. Certain regulations, such as the Internal Revenue Code (IRC), however, require specific useful lives to be used by regulation.

```
# Syntax: column-to-column
df1.merge(df2, how = 'inner'<d>, OR<on = col <d>, AND<left_on = col1, right_on = col2>>, sort = False <d>)

# Syntax: index-to-column/column-to-index
df1.merge(df2, how = 'inner'<d>, OR<AND<left_index = True, right_on = col2>, AND<left_on = col1, right_index = True>>, sort = False <d>)
```

```
# Regulatorily provided life of assets (estimates), except for appliances
reg_life = pd.DataFrame({'Category':['Land', 'Land Imp', 'Building', 'Equipment', 'F&F', 'Auto', 'Intangible'], 'Reg Life':['Inf', 15, 27.5, 5, 7, 5, 15]})

reg_life
```

Output:

	Category	Reg Life
0	Land	Inf
1	Land Imp	15
2	Building	27.5
3	Equipment	5
4	F&F	7

5	*Auto*	*5*
6	*Intangible*	*15*

To obtain a comparison between the assigned life and regulatory life of assets within the asset schedule, a left join should be performed: you want all records in the schedule to be returned, but nothing more or less.

If no join criterion is specified, the method defaults to an inner join on columns with the same name. Note that *merge()* does not have an *inplace* argument; the original variable is not updated unless overwritten with the new, merged dataframe.

```
fa.merge(reg_life, how = "left")                # Defaults to on = 'Category'
```

Output:

	Category	*Name*	*Price*	*Life*	*Yrly Depr*	*Reg Life*
0	*Land*	*Plot*	*300000*	*Inf*	*NA*	*Inf*
1	*Building*	*Office*	*150000*	*30*	*5000.0*	*27.5*
2	*Equipment*	*Roller*	*200000*	*5*	*40000.0*	*5*
3	*Equipment*	*Forklift*	*45000*	*7*	*6428.57*	*5*
4	*Appliance*	*Furnace*	*3500*	*10*	*350.0*	*NaN*
5	*F&F*	*Windows*	*7500*	*8*	*937.5*	*7*
6	*Building*	*Factory*	*350000*	*15*	*23333.33*	*27.5*
7	*Land Imp*	*Road*	*175000*	*20*	*8750.0*	*15*
8	*Auto*	*Car*	*22000*	*3*	*7333.33*	*5*

All records of the asset schedule are returned. Since the appliance category is not available in the regulatory life dataframe, record 4 is assigned NaN. Compare this to the below outputs for other types of joins.

```
fa.merge(reg_life)                # Defaults to join = 'inner'
```

Output:

	Category	*Name*	*Price*	*Life*	*Yrly Depr*	*Reg Life*
0	*Land*	*Plot*	*300000*	*Inf*	*NA*	*Inf*
1	*Building*	*Office*	*150000*	*30*	*5000.0*	*27.5*

2	*Equipment*	*Roller*	*200000*	*5*	*40000.0*	*5*
3	*Equipment*	*Forklift*	*45000*	*7*	*6428.57*	*5*
4	*F&F*	*Windows*	*7500*	*8*	*937.5*	*7*
5	*Building*	*Factory*	*350000*	*15*	*23333.33*	*27.5*
6	*Land Imp*	*Road*	*175000*	*20*	*8750.0*	*15*
7	*Auto*	*Car*	*22000*	*3*	*7333.33*	*5*

```
fa.merge(reg_life, how = "right")                    # Preserves right order
```

Output:	*Category*	*Name*	*Price*	*Life*	*Yrly Depr*	*Reg Life*
0	*Land*	*Plot*	*300000*	*Inf*	*NA*	*Inf*
1	*Land Imp*	*Road*	*175000*	*20*	*8750.0*	*15*
2	*Building*	*Office*	*150000*	*30*	*5000.0*	*27.5*
3	*Building*	*Factory*	*350000*	*15*	*23333.33*	*27.5*
4	*Equipment*	*Roller*	*200000*	*5*	*40000.0*	*5*
5	*Equipment*	*Forklift*	*45000*	*7*	*6428.57*	*5*
6	*F&F*	*Windows*	*7500*	*8*	*937.5*	*7*
7	*Auto*	*Car*	*22000*	*3*	*7333.33*	*5*
8	*Intangible*	*NaN*	*NaN*	*NaN*	*NaN*	*NaN*

```
fa.merge(reg_life, how = "outer")
```

Output:	*Category*	*Name*	*Price*	*Life*	*Yrly Depr*	*Reg Life*
0	*Land*	*Plot*	*300000*	*Inf*	*NA*	*Inf*
1	*Building*	*Office*	*150000*	*30*	*5000.0*	*27.5*
2	*Building*	*Factory*	*350000*	*15*	*23333.33*	*27.5*
3	*Equipment*	*Roller*	*200000*	*5*	*40000.0*	*5*
4	*Equipment*	*Forklift*	*45000*	*7*	*6428.57*	*5*
5	*Appliance*	*Furnace*	*3500*	*10*	*350.0*	*NaN*
6	*F&F*	*Windows*	*7500*	*8*	*937.5*	*7*
7	*Land Imp*	*Road*	*175000*	*20*	*8750.0*	*15*
8	*Auto*	*Car*	*22000*	*3*	*7333.33*	*5*
9	*Intangible*	*NaN*	*NaN*	*NaN*	*NaN*	*NaN*

df.join()

The *join()* method is much more restrictive than *merge()*. It can only join the index/column of the left dataframe to the index of the right dataframe. Effectively, then, the functionality of *join()* is covered by *merge()*. However, one crucial advantage of *join()* is that it allows for more than two dataframes to be joined in a single call, unlike *merge()*. Another advantage is that *join()* is faster and requires lesser arguments.

Remember, *join()* only supports index-to-index and column-to-index joins; it will always use the right dataframe's index, but may use either the index or a column of the left.

```
# Syntax: column-to-index
df1.join(df2, on = left_col, how = left' <d>, sort = False <d>)

# Syntax: index-to-index
df1.join(df2, how = 'left' <d>, sort = False <d>)
```

```
fa = fa.join(reg_life.set_index("Category"), on = "Category") #
set_index()
fa
```

Output:	*Category*	*Name*	*Price*	*Life*	*Yrly Depr*	*Reg Life*
0	*Land*	*Plot*	*300000*	*Inf*	*NA*	*Inf*
1	*Building*	*Office*	*150000*	*30*	*5000.0*	*27.5*
2	*Equipment*	*Roller*	*200000*	*5*	*40000.0*	*5*
3	*Equipment*	*Forklift*	*45000*	*7*	*6428.57*	*5*
4	*Appliance*	*Furnace*	*3500*	*10*	*350.0*	*NaN*
5	*F&F*	*Windows*	*7500*	*8*	*937.5*	*7*
6	*Building*	*Factory*	*350000*	*15*	*23333.33*	*27.5*
7	*Land Imp*	*Road*	*175000*	*20*	*8750.0*	*15*
8	*Auto*	*Car*	*22000*	*3*	*7333.33*	*5*

Note that the default join for the *join()* method is left, while the same for *merge()* is inner. You should remember this to avoid unintentional errors.

Aggregation in pandas

df.groupby()

You can use the *groupby()* method to aggregate items across either axis. The *groupby()* method in pandas is extremely broad. It can be used to perform one of the following:

- Splitting data into groups according to some criteria
- Applying a function independently to each group
- Combining the outcomes into a data structure.

Of the three, application of a function is the most common in business situations. Often, an aggregation function is used to summarize data along a specific axis. Common aggregation functions include *sum()*, *count()*, *mean()*, *min()*, *max()*, *first()*, and *last()*. Others include *std()* (standard deviation), *nth()* (n[th] value), and *describe()* (descriptive statistics).

```
# Syntax
df.groupby(by = col <d>, axis = "index" <d>, dropna = True <d>,
as_index = True <d>)
```

By default, the method will group along rows by the specified column(s) and return a *groupby* object with the grouping column as the index. You must apply an aggregation function to return the aggregated output. Assume that in the previous section on joins, the regulatory life was added to the fixed asset table using a left join.

```
fa.groupby("Category").sum()
```

Output:

	Price	*Yrly Depr*
Category		
Appliance	*3500*	*350.00*
Auto	*22000*	*7333.33*
Building	*500000*	*28333.33*
Equipment	*245000*	*46428.57*
F&F	*7500*	*937.50*
Land	*300000*	*0.00*
Land Imp	*175000*	*8750.00*

Note that only columns with all numeric values are aggregated. Also note that the Category column is returned as index of the new dataframe. You can change this, however.

```
fa.groupby("Reg Life", as_index = False).count()[["Reg Life",
"Category"]].rename(columns = {"Category":"count"})
```

Output:	*Reg Life*	*count*
0	*5.0*	*3*
1	*7.0*	*1*
2	*15.0*	*1*
3	*27.5*	*2*
4	*inf*	*1*

Grouping is too broad a topic to cover in a single chapter. Be sure to read the official pandas resource to understand this topic further: https://pandas.pydata.org/pandas-docs/stable/user_guide/groupby.html

Indexing

Indexing in pandas is very similar to filtering, except you can access specific "cells" in a dataframe by providing an index-column combination. As they are with most other Python objects, square brackets are used to index pandas dataframes. Two indexing methods are common.

df.iloc[]

You can use *iloc[]* to index dataframes by specifying integer positions. Subsets of rows and/or columns can be specified as part of a 0-indexed scale, running top-down for rows and left-right for columns.

```
# Syntax
df.iloc[row_slice, col_slice]
```

Several options are available for providing slices. You can provide single integer positions. For selecting multiple rows or columns, you can provide either a list of positions, or a slice object. You can also pass a Boolen array, which selects only True values.

You can access an individual value by providing its row-column positions.

```
fa.iloc[0, 3]                # Value at row 0 and column 3 (0-indexed)
```

Output: 'Inf'

If you index multiple positions of one dimension against a single position of the other, *iloc[]* returns a series. Indexing multiple positions of both dimensions returns a dataframe. Note that the distinction between single and multiple is syntactical, not numerical; a single position can be passed within a list and still be treated as multiple, returning a seriers/dataframe.

```
print(fa.iloc[[0,5], 2], "\n")        # Multiple rows. Returns series

print(fa.iloc[:9:2, [0, 5]], "\n")  # Slice object (dataframe). Returns dataframe

print(fa.iloc[[2],[4]])                # Single as multiple. Returns dataframe
```

Output:

```
0        300000
5        7500
Name: Price, dtype: int64

         Category      Reg Life
0        Land          Inf
2        Equipment     5
4        Appliance     NaN
6        Building      27.5
8        Auto          5

         Yrly Depr
2        40000.0
```

To return all values of a particular dimension, you can use a semicolon. For the column dimension, you can also omit the semicolon (not pass anything) to return all values. Specifying the semicolon is mandatory to return all rows.

```
print(fa.iloc[2], "\n")   # Returns 3rd row  across all columns, as series

print(fa.iloc[:, [3]])     # Returns 4th column across all rows, as dataframe
```

Output:

Category	*Equipment*
Name	*Roller*
Price	*200000*
Life	*5*
Yrly Depr	*40000.0*
Reg Life	*5*

Name: 2, dtype: object

	Life
0	*Inf*
1	*30*
2	*5*
3	*7*
4	*10*
5	*8*
6	*15*
7	*20*
8	*3*

Recall that the regulatory life of appliances was unavailable, and hence shows up as NaN in the dataframe. You can manually update it.

```
fa.iloc[4, 5] = 5
fa
```

Output:

	Category	*Name*	*Price*	*Life*	*Yrly Depr*	*Reg Lif*
0	*Land*	*Plot*	*300000*	*Inf*	*NA*	*Inf*
1	*Building*	*Office*	*150000*	*30*	*5000.0*	*27.5*
2	*Equipment*	*Roller*	*200000*	*5*	*40000.0*	*5*
3	*Equipment*	*Forklift*	*45000*	*7*	*6428.57*	*5*
4	*Appliance*	*Furnace*	*3500*	*10*	*350.0*	*5*
5	*F&F*	*Windows*	*7500*	*8*	*937.5*	*7*
6	*Building*	*Factory*	*350000*	*15*	*23333.33*	*27.5*
7	*Land Imp*	*Road*	*175000*	*20*	*8750.0*	*15*
8	*Auto*	*Car*	*22000*	*3*	*7333.33*	*5*

df.loc[]

You can use the *loc[]* method to index dataframes using row/column labels (as opposed to positions). Remember that if you do not explicitly pass one, pandas assigned a default incrementing index to the dataframe. In such a case, indexing rows with *loc[]* is the same as with *iloc[]*.

Except for using names instead of positions, all properties of *iloc[]* also apply to *loc[]*.

```
fa_index = fa.set_index("Category")                # Set "Category" as
index
fa_index
```

Output:	*Name*	*Price*	*Life*	*Yrly Depr*	*Reg Life*
Category					
Land	*Plot*	*300000*	*Inf*	*NA*	*Inf*
Building	*Office*	*150000*	*30*	*5000.0*	*27.5*
Equipment	*Roller*	*200000*	*5*	*40000.0*	*5*
Equipment	*Forklift*	*45000*	*7*	*6428.57*	*5*
Appliance	*Furnace*	*3500*	*10*	*350.0*	*5*
F&F	*Windows*	*7500*	*8*	*937.5*	*7*
Building	*Factory*	*350000*	*15*	*23333.33*	*27.5*
Land Imp	*Road*	*175000*	*20*	*8750.0*	*15*
Auto	*Car*	*22000*	*3*	*7333.33*	*5*

```
fa_index.loc["F&F", "Price"]
```

Output: 7500

If a label repeats in either dimension, the selection is treated as a multiple index and a series/dataframe is returned.

```
fa_index.loc["Building", "Price"]                  # Returns series
```

Output: Category
Building 150000
Building 350000
Name: Price, dtype: int64

```
fa_index.loc[["Equipment", "Auto"]]
```

Output:

	Name	Price	Life	Yrly Depr	Reg Life
Category					
Equipment	*Roller*	*200000*	*5*	*40000.0*	*5*
Equipment	*Forklift*	*45000*	*7*	*6428.57*	*5*
Auto	*Car*	*22000*	*3*	*7333.33*	*5*

```
fa_index.loc[:, "Name":"Reg Life":2]          # Every other column
```

Output:

	Name	Life	Reg Life
Category			
Land	*Plot*	*Inf*	*Inf*
Building	*Office*	*30*	*27.5*
Equipment	*Roller*	*5*	*5*
Equipment	*Forklift*	*7*	*5*
Appliance	*Furnace*	*10*	*5*
F&F	*Windows*	*8*	*7*
Building	*Factory*	*15*	*27.5*
Land Imp	*Road*	*20*	*15*
Auto	*Car*	*3*	*5*

Input/Output (IO)

Microsoft Excel is widely used in business. Support for working with Excel files is strong in Python. In pandas, you can import spreadsheets as dataframes. Once imported, you can work with them as you would with an internally created dataframe.

Different methods exist to respectively work with core Excel files (.xlsx, .xls, etc.) and other delimited files (.csv, .txt, etc.).

Importing Excel Files

You can use the *read_excel()* method to read in core Excel files as pandas dataframes. Formats supported include xls, xlsx, xlsm, xlsb, and other software-specific extensions.

The *read_excel()* method is one of the broadest I have seen. There are a host of arguments you can pass to correctly import your Excel file. For example, you can specify which row in the spreadsheet to read data from, whether there is a header row, whether there are specific data types to be assigned to certain columns, and whether some rows need to be skipped from import. Be sure to check out the official documentation for all arguments you can pass.

```
# Syntax
pd.read_excel(path, sheet_name = 0 <d>, header = 0 <d>, dtype =
None <d>, skiprows = None <d>, nrows = None <d>)
```

By default, the method will import all rows from the first sheet (tab) in the Excel file considering the first row as a header without skipping any rows from the top. You can change any of these arguments.

```
path = "C:/Users/uname/Desktop/file.xlsx"

# Default
pd.read_excel(path)

# Set row 6 (0-indexed) as header/column
pd.read_excel(path, header = 5)

# Set sixth row (row 6) as header and import rows 7 – 1006
pd.read_excel(path, header = 5, nrows = 1000)

# Set row 2 as header, skip next six rows, and import ten rows after
that
pd.read_excel(path, header = 1, skip rows = 6, nrows = 10)

# Import sheet 3 (0-indexed)
pd.read_excel(path, sheet_name = 2)

# Import all sheets in a dictionary. Format {sheet_name:dataframe}
pd.read_excel(path, sheet_name = None)

# Import sheet named "sheet1", sheet 3, and the last sheet
pd.read_excel(path, sheet_name = ["sheet1", 3, -1])
```

```
# Set first column as index and skip rows 2, 4, 6
pd.read_excel(path, index_col = 0, skiprows = [1, 3, 5])

# Import all columns of first sheet (sheet 1) as text/string
pd.read_excel(path, dtype = str)

# Import 'col1' as string, 'col2' as float, and infer type for other
columns
pd.read_excel(path, dtype = {'col1':str, 'col2':float})

# Import first 50 columns (0-indexed as 0 – 49)
pd.read_excel(path, usecols = [col for col in range(50)])
```

Note that the backslash (\) has a special connotation in the context of Python strings. The backslash is used to denote special characters, such as newline (\n) and tab (\t). When passing file paths, hence, you cannot pass traditional paths with backslashes. You have two options here:

1. Convert all backslashes in the path to forward slashes (/).
2. "Escape" the backslash's special status by formatting the string as a "raw" string. This simply means adding "r" as a prefix to the string. A raw string considers backslashes as literals and not special characters. For example, "C:/Users/uname/Desktop/file.xlsx" is equivalent to r"C:\Users\uname\Desktop\file.xlsx".

There are many arguments and many variations possible with *read_excel()*. Again, the documentation is your ally.

Importing Delimited Files

The *read_csv()* method can be used to import files with any delimiter (the name can be misleading). Most commonly, if files are delimited, they are comma-delimited. Many arguments exist to correctly import your delimited file.

```
# Syntax
pd.read_csv(path, sep = ',' <d>, header = 'infer' <d>, dtype = None
<d>, skiprows = None <d>, nrows = None <d>))
```

Importing works much the same way as for core Excel files, with a few obvious modifications.

```
path = r"C:\Users\uname\Desktop\file.csv"

# Default
pd.read_csv(path)

# Import tab-delimited file
pd.read_csv(path, sep = '\t')

# Delimiters in strings within quotechar will be ignored
pd.read_csv(path, quotechar = "#")
```

Exporting Files

You can export pandas dataframes as Excel or delimited files. Note that the export methods are dataframe methods, whereas the import methods are library methods.

Relevant methods are *to_excel()* and *to_csv()*.

```
# Syntax: Single sheet
df.to_excel(path, sheet_name = "sheet1" <d>, header = True <d>,
index = True <d>)

# Syntax: Multiple sheets
with pd.ExcelWriter(path) as writer:
        df1.to_excel(writer, sheet_name = "sheet1")
        df2.to_excel(writer, sheet_name = "sheet2")

        dn.to_excel(writer, sheet_name = "sheetn")
```

The default export is a single sheet named "sheet1" with a header row and index column. Exporting multiple sheets simultaneously to a single file requires instantiating an *ExcelWriter* object using the *with* statement.

```
# Create new or overwrite existing file
path = r"C:\Users\uname\Desktop\new_file.xlsx"

# Default
df.to_excel(path)

# Export single sheet as "new_sheet" without index
df.to_excel(path, sheet_name = 'new_sheet', index = False)
```

```
# Export only two specific columns
df.to_excel(path, columns = ["col1", "col2"])

# Export two dataframes as two sheets in a single workbook
with pd.ExcelWriter(path) as w:
        df1.to_excel(w, sheet_name = '1st_sheet', index = False)
        df2.to_excel(w, sheet_name = '2nd_sheet', columns = ["abc",
"def"])
```

The *to_csv()* method can export delimited files in a variety of formats.

```
# Syntax
df.to_csv(path, sep = ",", header = True <d>, index = True <d>)
```

```
path = r"C:\Users\uname\Desktop\new_file.csv"

# Default
df.to_csv(path)

# Export double tab-delimited
df.to_csv(path, sep = "\t\t")

# Export pipe-delimited text file
df.to_csv(path.replace('csv', 'txt'), sep = "|")
```

Miscellaneous pandas

The following pandas attributes and methods do not fall into any particular category, but I have found myself using them at one point or another.

df.shape

This attribute returns the shape of a dataframe as a tuple of the number of rows and columns.

```
fa.shape                    # 9 rows, 6 columns
```

Output: (9, 6)

df.index/df.columns

These attributes respectively return the index and columns as iterables.

```
print("Index:", fa.index)
print("Columns:", fa.columns)
```

Output: Index: Int64Index([0, 1, 2, 3, 4, 5, 6, 7, 8], dtype='int64')
Columns: Index(['Category', 'Name', 'Price', 'Life', 'Yrly Depr', 'Reg Life'], dtype='object')

df.head()

This method returns the first n (5 by default) records of a series or data frame. There is also the *tail()* method, which returns the last n rows (5 by default).

```
fa.head(6)
```

Output:	*Category*	*Name*	*Price*	*Life*	*Yrly Depr*	*Reg Life*
0	*Land*	*Plot*	*300000*	*Inf*	*NA*	*Inf*
1	*Building*	*Office*	*150000*	*30*	*5000.0*	*27.5*
2	*Equipment*	*Roller*	*200000*	*5*	*40000.0*	*5*
3	*Equipment*	*Forklift*	*45000*	*7*	*6428.57*	*5*
4	*Appliance*	*Furnace*	*3500*	*10*	*350.0*	*NaN*
5	*F&F*	*Windows*	*7500*	*8*	*937.5*	*7*

df.nsmallest()/df.nlargest()

These methods return the first n smallest or largest values respectively, sorted by a specified column.

```
fa.nsmallest(2, "Price")          # Smallest two prices
```

Output:	*Category*	*Name*	*Price*	*Life*	*Yrly Depr*	*Reg Life*
4	*Appliance*	*Furnace*	*3500*	*10*	*350.0*	*NaN*
5	*F&F*	*Windows*	*7500*	*8*	*937.5*	*7*

df.sort_values()

This method will sort a dataframe, by default, using a column and in ascending order.

```
fa.sort_values(by = "Price", ascending = False)
```

Output:	*Category*	*Name*	*Price*	*Life*	*Yrly Depr*	*Reg Life*
6	*Building*	*Factory*	*350000*	*15*	*23333.33*	*27.5*
0	*Land*	*Plot*	*300000*	*Inf*	*NA*	*Inf*
2	*Equipment*	*Roller*	*200000*	*5*	*40000.0*	*5*
7	*Land Imp*	*Road*	*175000*	*20*	*8750.0*	*15x*
1	*Building*	*Office*	*150000*	*30*	*5000.0*	*27.5*
3	*Equipment*	*Forklift*	*45000*	*7*	*6428.57*	*5*
8	*Auto*	*Car*	*22000*	*3*	*7333.33*	*5*
5	*F&F*	*Windows*	*7500*	*8*	*937.5*	*7*
4	*Appliance*	*Furnace*	*3500*	*10*	*350.0*	*NaN*

df.rename()

This method will rename one or more columns, by default. It can also rename rows, but that is not used as often.

```
fa.rename(columns = {"Name":"N", "Life":"L"})
```

Output:	*Category*	*N*	*Price*	*L*	*Yrly Depr*	*Reg Life*
0	*Land*	*Plot*	*300000*	*Inf*	*NA*	*Inf*
1	*Building*	*Office*	*150000*	*30*	*5000.0*	*27.5*
2	*Equipment*	*Roller*	*200000*	*5*	*40000.0*	*5*
3	*Equipment*	*Forklift*	*45000*	*7*	*6428.57*	*5*
4	*Appliance*	*Furnace*	*3500*	*10*	*350.0*	*NaN*
5	*F&F*	*Windows*	*7500*	*8*	*937.5*	*7*
6	*Building*	*Factory*	*350000*	*15*	*23333.33*	*27.5*
7	*Land Imp*	*Road*	*175000*	*20*	*8750.0*	*15*
8	*Auto*	*Car*	*22000*	*3*	*7333.33*	*5*

```
# Rename all columns to only the first letter and update inplace
fa.rename(columns = {col:col[0] for col in fa.columns}, inplace = True)
fa
```

Output:	C	N	P	L	Y	R
0	*Land*	*Plot*	*300000*	*Inf*	*NA*	*Inf*
1	*Building*	*Office*	*150000*	*30*	*5000.0*	*27.5*
2	*Equipment*	*Roller*	*200000*	*5*	*40000.0*	*5*
3	*Equipment*	*Forklift*	*45000*	*7*	*6428.57*	*5*
4	*Appliance*	*Furnace*	*3500*	*10*	*350.0*	*NaN*
5	*F&F*	*Windows*	*7500*	*8*	*937.5*	*7*
6	*Building*	*Factory*	*350000*	*15*	*23333.33*	*27.5*
7	*Land Imp*	*Road*	*175000*	*20*	*8750.0*	*15*
8	*Auto*	*Car*	*22000*	*3*	*7333.33*	*5*

pandas is the backbone of your data analysis work in Python. It is also the tool you will almost always use to import Excel files. For many coders, it is a default import at the start of any code. Storing data in the powerful pandas dataframes allows for the application of other libraries to the data in easy iterations. Read the official pandas documentation to install and learn more about this library

https://pandas.pydata.org/docs/

NUMPY

NumPy is an array-processing library used in scientific computing and storing multi-dimensional data. Arrays refer to some type of tabular data where each element has a positive integer index (much like in a pandas dataframe).

NumPy is an important library for scientific work. In general, NumPy arrays are much faster than either pandas series or dataframes and support faster numerical calculations. NumPy arrays are also the default input of many advanced machine learning algorithms. Certain other advanced algorithms, such as those pertaining to computer vision, also represent images as NumPy arrays.

However, I have found its utility to be limited in business. Most, if not all, of your requirements should be satisfied by pandas. From a business perspective, most of your tasks will revolve around IO operations, looping over for automations, data analysis, etc. pandas is great for all these tasks.

```
import numpy as np

arr1 = np.array([9, 8, 7])
print ("Rank 1 Array: \n", arr1)

arr2 = np.array([[9, 8, 7],
                 [3, 2, 1]])
print ("Rank 2 Array: \n", arr2)

arr_tup = np.array((9, 8, 7))
print ("\nArray using passed tuple:\n", arr_tup)
```

Output: Rank 1 Array:

[9 8 7]

Rank 2 Array:

[[9 8 7]
[3 2 1]]

Array using passed tuple:

[9 8 7]

I have not included include more information on NumPy because, again, I have found it to be of little use. I do want you to know that it exists. It contains some useful arithmetic methods, but most of them can be replicated easily in pandas. For advanced ML or computer vision tasks, however, NumPy arrays are a staple because they are lighter than pandas data structures. There is plenty of information available online for you to delve deeper into arrays.

Read NumPy's documentation to install and learn more about this library: https://numpy.org/doc/stable

OS

The os module is part of Python's standard suite of libraries (you do not need to install it separately). It is a powerful module that allows you to directly interact with the operating system. The module provides various portable functionalities independent of the underlying operating system (meaning you can control Mac and Windows alike).

I use os primarily to:

- Import names of files in a folder
- Create new files or folders
- Rename or delete files or folders

The library has many other uses. Note that in the context of os, the terms "folder" and "directory" are sometimes used interchangeably.

Retrieving the Current Working Directory

The Current Working Directory (CWD) is the location on your system where Python programs are executed. This is usually separate from the location where your Python file is "physically" saved.

If a file is saved in the CWD, you can call it directly by name (without specifying the entire path).

```
import pandas as pd

# If Desktop is not CWD
pd.read_csv(r"C:\Users\uname\Desktop\new_file.csv")

# If Desktop is CWD
pd.read_csv("new_file.csv")
```

You can get the CWD using *getcwd()*, and update it using the *chdir()* method.

```
import os

print("Old CWD:", os.getcwd())
os.chdir(r"C:\Users\uname\Desktop")
print ("New CWD:", os.getcwd())
```

Output: Old CWD: C:\Users\uname
New CWD: C:\Users\uname\Desktop

Listing Files and Directories

You can use the *listdir()* method to return a list containing names of files and folders at a specified path. This is frequently used in conjunction with other operations that need to be performed on files within a directory. The *listdir()* method returns file names with extensions. It is important to note that, while it will often match the underlying directory's, the order of items returned by *listdir()* is arbitrary.

The method returns a list of strings. Once imported, you can modify the list and the file names using all list and string methods.

```
path = "C:/Users/uname/Desktop"

path_dir = os.listdir(path)
print ("Desktop content:\n", path_dir)
```

Output: Desktop content:
['file1.jpg', 'file2.pdf', 'file3.pdf', 'file4.xlsx', 'folder1', 'system.ini']

Another method, called *walk()*, returns the entire tree of the specified directory (all files, folders, files in those folders, etc.). Check out the documentation for details.

Creating Directories

You can create folders using the *mkdir()* and *makedirs()* methods. Both methods are very similar, except *makedirs()* also creates any intermediate directories that do not exist. Because *mkdir()* is effectively a subset of *makedirs()*, I usually use the latter.

Assume that you want to save your tax returns. You want to create a separate folder for each year within a master folder.

```
os.mkdir("C:/Users/uname/Desktop/Tax Returns/2021")
```

Output: FileNotFoundError: [WinError 3] The system cannot find the path specified: 'C:/Users/uname/Desktop/Tax Returns/2021'

The above throws an error because the method cannot create the folder 2021 when there is no folder called Tax Returns. You can solve this problem by using *makedirs()*, which will return nothing and create 2021 and all intermediate directories.

```
os.makedirs("C:/Users/chibb/Desktop/Tax Returns/2021")
```

Renaming and Deleting

You can use the *rename()* and *remove()* methods to rename and delete, respectively. Note that *remove()* can only delete files, not folders.

```
# Syntax
os.rename(old_path, new_path)
os.remove(path_to_delete)
```

Remember, files/folders in the CWD can be specified with only their names, while those at other locations need to be specified with their full paths. Since you will rarely save or download files to the CWD, *path.join()* (covered next) makes renaming and deleting very efficient.

```
# File is in CWD
os.rename("weird_download_name.pdf", "name_convention.pdf")

# File is elsewhere
os.rename(os.path.join(folder_path, "weird_download_name.pdf"),
os.path.join(folder_path, "new_name_convention.pdf"))
```

You can delete folders using the *rmdir()* and *removedirs()* methods. The former will delete only the deepest directory whereas the latter will recursively delete all intermediate directories. As opposed to when creating directories, I usually use the *rmdir()* method when deleting. This is because recursively deleting directories is more "dangerous" than creating them. Note that both methods only work with folders that are empty. If you have files within a folder, use *remove()* to delete them before deleting the folder.

```
# Deletes 2021
os.rmdir("C:/Users/uname/Desktop/Tax Returns/2021")

# Not recommended
```

```
os.removedirs("C:/Users/uname/Desktop/Tax Returns/2021")
```

Extending Paths

File paths can quickly get complicated. When working with your operating system, you will need to add to current paths to create new files and folders. For example, if the Desktop path is "C:/Users/uname/Desktop" and you want to create a new folder containing a new file, you will need to add a "/", followed by the new folder name, followed by another "/", followed by the new file name; ("C:/Users/uname/Desktop/new_folder/new_file").

When working with many files, creating new paths can quickly become tedious. You can use the *path.join()* method to efficiently extend paths. This is very handy when renaming files, especially those that are downloaded as part of an automation.

```
path = r"C:\Users\uname\Desktop"

print(os.path.join(path, "tax_records.csv"))
print(os.path.join(path, "pension_docs", "benefits.docx"))
```

Output: C:\Users\uname\Desktop\tax_records.csv
C:\Users\uname\Desktop\pension_docs\benefits.docx

As an example, assume that your Python automation downloads invoices in .pdf format. You want to rename all invoices with a standard name followed by an identifying integer, and want to delete any files that are not in .pdf format. Study the solution below that uses four os methods, a string method, and f-string formatting.

```
path = r"C:\Users\uname\Desktop\downloaded_invoices"
file_list = os.listdir(path)

counter = 1                          # Initialize a counter
for file in file_list:
        if file.endswith(".pdf"):
                os.rename(os.path.join(path, file), os.path.join(path,
                                f"new_file_{counter}.pdf"))
                counter += 1         # Increment counter
```

```
        else:
                os.remove(os.path.join(path, file))
```

Read os' documentation to install and learn more about this library: https://docs.python.org/3/library/os.html

SHUTIL

Shutil has much overlap with os. Both modules are used for file operations. Shutil is a higher-level library designed to combine methods of low-level Python libraries. It aims to reduce the amount of code needed for operations.

The primary use of shutil in my codes is to move (cut) or copy. Relevant methods include *move()* and *copy()*, respectively. The syntax mimics that of *os.rename()*. Note the important distinction that these shutil methods perform the system operation <u>and</u> return the new path as string (which can be assigned to a variable). The os methods only complete the operation and return nothing.

```
import shutil

source = "path/folder_1/myfile.py"              # Existing file
destination = "path/folder_2/myfile2.py"        # Doesn't exist yet

dest = shutil.copy(source, destination)         # Perform copy
print(dest)                                     # Print new path
```

Output: path/folder_2/myfile2.py

If a file with the specified name already exists at the destination, it is replaced with the newly written file. Also, note that *copy()* will only copy the content of a file, not its metadata (for example, the author name and title of a Word document). The *move()* method works similarly, except it cuts a file to the destination.

Other useful methods within shutil include the following:

1. *copy2()*: Copy file content <u>and</u> metadata
2. *copytree()*: Replicate directories
3. *rmtree()*: Remove directories
4. *which()*: Locate applications

Read shutil's documentation to install and learn more about this library: https://docs.python.org/3/library/shutil.html

ZIPFILE

Files in ZIP format are used to compress and store other files and folders. These files normally end with .zip and support lossless compression: the combined size of the contents reduces without any loss of data. You can use the zipfile module in Python to work with ZIP files.

You can create, modify, and extract ZIP files. In general, these operations are also possible by manually selecting multiple ZIP files together and then right clicking for a bunch of extraction options. The power of the zipfile module is evident when using it in conjunction with other Python structures to dynamically select files based on certain criteria and then zipping them.

The zipfile module's class ZipFile contains the most useful methods. By default, your import is going to be just this class and you are going to work with a ZipFile object.

```
from zipfile import ZipFile
path_z = r"C:\Users\uname\Desktop\fund_data.zip"  # Existing zip

# Extract one file. Mode 'r' to read
with Zipfile(path_z, mode = 'r') as zip:          # Create ZipFile object
        zip.extract("fund_assets.xlsx", path =
r"C:\Users\uname\Desktop")

# Extract all files. Mode 'r' is default
with Zipfile(path_z) as zip:
        zip.extractall(path = r"C:\Users\uname\Desktop")

# Extract multiple files
with Zipfile(path_z) as zip:
        zip.extract(members = ["fund_assets.xlsx",
"fund_liabilities.xlsx"],  path = r"C:\Users\uname\Desktop")
        writer_zip.write(path_file_3)
```

Note the use of the *with* statement. This unique statement in Python is used as a "context manager." Certain types of IO operations require you to open, work on, and then close files. Not following these steps in order renders unintended results. These steps can be avoided by including operations in a *with* statement. The *with* statement is one of the more confusing ones out there, so do not fret too much over it.

```
from zipfile import ZipFile
path_z_n = r"C:\Users\uname\Desktop\new_data.zip"        # New
zip
path_file_1 =
r"C:\Users\uname\Desktop\files_to_add\new_file1.txt"
path_file_2 =
r"C:\Users\uname\Desktop\files_to_add\new_file2.jpg"
path_file_3 =
r"C:\Users\uname\Desktop\files_to_add\new_file3.pdf"

# Add files to zip. Mode 'w' to write
with Zipfile(path_z, mode = 'w') as writer_zip:
        writer_zip.write(path_file_1)
        writer_zip.write(path_file_2)
        writer_zip.write(path_file_3)
```

When creating ZIP files, zipfile will not compress the added files by default. You will have to specify a compression protocol to the *compression* argument of the ZipFile object. Each protocol except for the default "only storage, no compression" requires installation of an additional module.

Read zipfile's documentation to install and learn more about this library: https://docs.python.org/3/library/zipfile.html

THEFUZZ

Several situations arise in accounting and business when textual data must be compared. You may want to deduplicate workpaper entries, conduct bank reconciliations (compare bank statements to internal books), rename files, or compare invoices to receiving reports (ascertain that only what was received has been billed). In general, if you are dealing with large amounts of similar data from multiple sources, you may want to compare for inaccuracies, discrepancies, or simply to determine which source is better suited to your needs.

However, you will rarely find that two strings are exactly equal. There will likely be unwanted characters, word-order discrepancies, or case issues (python vs. PYTHON). Fuzzy string matching is an umbrella of techniques that mathematically establish "equivalency" (not equality) between strings. Fuzzy methods can be used to match textual data that is not technical equal, but intuitively equivalent.

You can use the thefuzz library (formerly known as fuzzywuzzy) to apply a range of fuzzy matching algorithms. The underlying technicality: thefuzz uses Levenshtein Distance (LD) to establish similarity between two strings. LD equals the minimum number of single character edits that are required to change either of the two strings into the other. An edit can refer to a character's insertion, deletion, or replacement. What you need to remember, however, is that the library is designed to provide you with an equivalency ratio, between 1 and 100, for two strings. This is known as the LD Ratio (LDR).

The library contains multiple mathematical ratios, and your choice depends on your data.

- *fuzz.ratio():* LDR for strings to exactly match. The default choice.
- *fuzz.partial_ratio()*: Maximum LDR for the shorter string to match any subset of the longer string (without changing word-order) whose length equals the shorter string's.
- *fuzz.token_sort_ratio()*: Sort tokens in both strings after converting to lowercase and then calculate LDR, making comparison independent of word-order.

- *fuzz.token_set_ratio()*: Equivalent to *token_sort_ratio()*, except repeating tokens are not considered.
- *fuzz.WRatio()*: A weighted combination of the previous four ratios.

```
from thefuzz import fuzz

s1 = "Python for Business"
s2 = "It is important to learn Python for Business"

print("FW Ratio:", fuzz.ratio(s1, s2))
print("FW PartialRatio:", fuzz.partial_ratio(s1, s2))
print("FW TokenSortRatio:", fuzz.token_sort_ratio(s1, s2))
print("FW TokenSetRatio:", fuzz.token_set_ratio(s1, s2))
print("FW WRatio:", fuzz.WRatio(s1, s2))
```

Output: FW Ratio: 60
FW PartialRatio: 100
FW TokenSortRatio: 60
FW TokenSetRatio: 100
FW WRatio: 90

process

You can use the *process* module within thefuzz library to compare a given string to multiple strings and return all LDRs simultaneously. The *extract()* method returns a list of tuples with all LDRs and corresponding strings, whereas *extractOne()* returns a tuple containing only the maximum LDR with the corresponding string.

```
# Syntax: extract
process.extract(string, list_of_strings, scorer = fuzz.WRatio <d>, limit = None <d>)

# Syntax: extractOne
process.extractOne(string, list_of_strings, scorer = fuzz.WRatio <d>)
```

By default, both methods return a weighted combination of all four ratios for all strings. You can change the scorer of either method depending on the structure of your strings.

```
from thefuzz import process

string = 'python for accounting and business'
list_of_strings = ['Python for Business', 'python business', 'p. for B']

print("All ratios:", process.extract(string, list_of_strings))
print("Best one:", process.extractOne(string, list_of_strings))
```

Output: All ratios: [('Python for Business', 86), ('python business', 86), ('p. for B', 86)]   Best one: ('Python for Business', 86)

Clearly, the default *fuzz.WRatio()* is not the best scorer for this scenario.

```
string = 'python for accounting and business'
list_of_strings = ['Python for Business', 'python business', 'p. for B']

print("Top 2:", process.extract(string, list_of_strings, scorer =
fuzz.ratio, limit = 2))                # Only return top 2
print("Best one:", process.extractOne(string, list_of_strings, scorer =
fuzz.ratio))
```

Output: Top 2: [('Python for Business', 72), ('python business', 61)]
Best one: ('Python for Business', 72)

Read thefuzz's documentation to install and learn more about this library: https://github.com/seatgeek/thefuzz. Also check out examples at https://www.geeksforgeeks.org/fuzzywuzzy-python-library

PYJOKES

What is life without some whimsy! You can use the pyjokes library to generate short jokes. You can either return a single joke at random using the *get_joke()* method or a list of jokes using *get_jokes()*. Both methods accept two arguments: language and category.

Available languages are English (en), German (de), Spanish (es), Italian (it), Galician (gl), and Basque (eu). Available categories are general (neutral), Chuck Norris-related jokes (chuck), and any random joke (all).

```
import pyjokes

one_joke = pyjokes.get_joke(language = "en", category = "chuck")
        print(one_joke)

two_jokes = pyjokes.get_jokes(language = "en", category = "neutral")
for i in range(2):
        print(two_jokes[i])
```

Output: Code runs faster when Chuck Norris watches it.
Why did the programmer quit his job? Because he didn't get arrays.
A programmer was found dead in the shower.
Next to their body was a bottle of shampoo with the instructions 'Lather, Rinse and Repeat'.

Read pyjokes' documentation to install and learn more about this library: https://pypi.org/project/pyjokes

CHAPTER 07 | **CASE STUDIES**

Below are some business use-cases for Python. As you go through them, pay particular attention to how different concepts presented thus far in the book can be used together to create comprehensive, end-to-end solutions for specific business problems.

The codes shown below are complicated and can seem daunting at first. Take your time and break each solution into chunks of code. Move on to the next chunk when you understand the previous one. Consult previous chapters (and the internet) as needed.

Case 1

An auditor downloads 1,500 files from the client's online portal. Each file falls in one of two categories. One includes .jpg files for inventory counts at client stores in either Texas (TX), Louisiana (LA), or Mississippi (MS). The other includes vendor invoices in .pdf format. The inventory count files have their respective state's name in their file names, although there is no consistent format. Some vendor invoices have their file names as numeric codes.

The auditor needs to separate inventory counts from vendor invoices. In addition, inventory counts need to be grouped by state and all vendor invoices except for those with a numeric code need to be grouped together.

```
import os
import shutil
import zipfile

path = r"C:\Users\uname\Desktop\pbc_files"    # provided by client
all_files = os.listdir(path)

os.makedirs(os.path.join(path, "Vendor Invoices", "Numeric"))

for folder in ("TX", "LA", "MS"):
```

```
        os.makedirs(os.path.join(path, "Inventory Counts", folder))

for file in all_files:
        if file.endswith("jpg"):
                if ("tx" in file.lower()) or ("texas" in file.lower()):
                        shutil.move(os.path.join(path, file), os.path.join
                        (path, "Inventory Counts", "TX", file))
                elif ("la" in file.lower()) or ("louisiana" in file.lower()):
                        shutil.move(os.path.join(path, file), os.path.join
                        (path,  "Inventory Counts", "LA", file))
                elif ("ms" in file.lower()) or ("mississippi" in file.lower()):
                        shutil.move(os.path.join(path, file), os.path.join
                        (path,  "Inventory Counts", "MS", file))

        else:
                if file.rstrip(".pdf").isnumeric():
                        shutil.move(os.path.join(path, file), os.path.join
                        (path, "Vendor Invoices", "Numeric", file))
                else:
                        shutil.move(os.path.join(path, file), os.path.join
                        (path, "Vendor Invoices", file))
```

Case 2

A company is determining the annual bonus for its employees. The base rate for bonus is 8% of annual salary. For every additional five-year tenure, the bonus increases by 2%, up to a combined maximum increment of 12% (a bonus of 20%). After calculations, the company must send each employee an email with their bonus information.

Two Excel files are available: the first file contains employees' unique ID, annual salary, and tenure. Columns are named as follows: ID, Salary, and Tenure. Bonus is awarded by default unless specifically instructed otherwise due to low performance. Such employees have the text "No Bonus" in the Salary column. Data starts on row 2 in this file. The second file contains employee unique ID, first name, and last name. Columns are named as follows: Key, First Name, and Last Name. Data starts on row 1 in this file.

```
import pandas as pd
```

```
sal_data =
pd.read_excel(r"C:\Users\uname\Desktop\employee_salary.xlsx",
header =                    1)
name_data =
pd.read_excel(r"C:\Users\uname\Desktop\employee_names.xlsx")

merged = sal_data.merge(name_data, how = "left", left_on = "ID",
right_on                                    = "Key").drop(columns =
"Key")
bonus_list = []

for sal, ten in zip(merged["Salary"], merged["Tenure"]):
        try:
                bonus = sal * min((8 + (ten//5 * 2)), 20)/100
        except TypeError:
                bonus = "No Bonus"

        bonus_list.append(bonus)

merged["Bonus"] = bonus_list

email_list = []
for first, last, bonus in zip(merged["ID"], merged["First Name"],
                                        merged["Last Name"],
merged["Bonus"]):
        if bonus != "No Bonus":
                email = f"""Dear {last}, {first}
                Your annual bonus for the year ended December 31,
                2021 equals ${bonus}. Please review your online
                portal for details.

                        Sincerely,
                        Management"""

        else:
                email = "No email required"

        email_list.append(email)
```

```
merged["Email Draft"] = email_list

merged.to_excel(r"C:\Users\uname\Desktop\employee_bonus_calcs.
xlsx",                              index = False)
```

Case 3

(Note: This is a complicated string manipulation case. Pay particular attention as you go over.)

Investment fund ABC entirely invests in other funds (commonly called a "fund of funds"). ABC wants to calculate the Net Asset Value (NAV) of all its "invested" funds. Assume that the NAV (calculated as the Assets - Liabilities/# Shares Outstanding) is not directly reported by funds in their annual report. ABC has holding in 600 funds. Instead of manually going through each annual report and calculating the NAV, the fund wants to automate this process.

Thankfully, all invested funds report key figures in a standardized format on page 10 in their annual report. Using OCR, ABC has extracted text from all page 10's as Python strings. ABC now must extract the numerical figure, which appear with comma separators, from each string. Assume that ABC has stored the parsed strings as dictionary values, with fund name as keys.

```
# Assume txt_dict exists
# Assets format: "Total assets are $num, in nominal terms"
# Liabilities format: "Amount owed equals $num in liabilities"
# Number of Shares format: "Fund had num shares outstanding"

nav_list = []

for fund, text in txt_dict.items():
        assets = float(text[text.find("Total assets are") + 18:text.find(",",
                        text.find("Total assets are"))].replace(",", ""))

        liabs = float(text[text.find("Amount owed equals") +
20:text.find                        (" in liabilities")].replace(",", ""))
```

```
        shares = float(text[text.rfind("Fund had", text.find(" shares
                        outstanding")) + 9:text.find(" shares
                        outstanding")].replace(",", ""))

        nav = (assets - liabs)/shares
        nav_list.append([fund, nav])              # List of lists

nav_frame = pd.DataFrame(nav_list, columns = ["Fund Name", "NAV"])
nav_frame.to_excel(r"C:\Users\uname\Desktop\nav_data.xlsx", index = False)
```

Case 4

Month-end bank reconciliation is in process. There are over 1,000 transactions to be reviewed. Since multiple entries can have the same amount, a staff member usually matches bank statement and journal entry descriptions manually. Obviously, descriptions on both sides are rarely the same. Transactions that do not reconcile are analyzed separately until at least 95% of all transactions are explained for. The 5% or less discrepancy is considered immaterial. Any bank transactions with the word "Subtotal" in their description should be ignored. This process needs to now be automated within a Python function.

Bank statement data can be exported from the bank's website as a tab-delimited file. Journal entry data exists in an Excel file. Since descriptions on but sides are similar but not the same, fuzzy matching can be used to establish equivalency.

```
import pandas as pd
from thefuzz import process


def recon():
        """This function will perform a bank reconciliation.
        Column names must remain standard. Function output can be
        assigned to variable."""

        bank = pd.read_csv(input("Provide path to bank statement: "),
sep =                               "\t")
        je = pd.read_excel(input("Provide path to bank statement: "))
```

```
        # Bank file columns: Date, Description, Debit, Credit
        # JE file columns: Date, Accounts, Debit, Credit, Description

        bank_match_list = [process.extractOne(desc1,
je.Description)[0] if
        process.extractOne(desc1, je.Description)[1]
                > 90 else "No Match" for desc1 in [desc1 for
                        desc1 in bank.Description if "subtotal" not in
                                desc1.lower()]]

        je_match_list = [process.extractOne(desc2,
bank.Description)[0] if
        process.extractOne(desc2, bank.Description)[1] > 90
                else "No Match" for desc2 in [desc2 for desc2 in
                        je.Description if "subtotal" not in desc2.lower()]]

        bank["JE Match"] = bank_match_list
        bank["Absolute Amount"] = [abs(dr1) if dr1 != 0 else abs(cr1)
for                                         dr1, cr1 in
zip(bank.Debit,
        bank.Credit)]

        je["Bank Match"] = je_match_list
        je["Absolute Amount"] = [abs(dr2) if dr2 != 0 else abs(cr2) for
dr2,                                        cr2 in zip(je.Debit,
je.Credit)]

        bank_unmatched = bank[bank["JE Match"] == "No
                                        Match"].sort_values(by =
"Absolute                                           Amount",
ascending = False)

        je_unmatched = je[je["Bank Match"] == "No
Match"].sort_values(by                      = "Absolute Amount",
ascending = False)

        bank_unmatched =
bank_unmatched[bank_unmatched["Absolute
                Amount"].cumsum()/bank["Absolute
                        Amount"].sum() <= .95]
```

```
        je_unmatched = je_unmatched[je_unmatched["Absolute
                                    Amount"].cumsum()/je["Absolute
Amount"].sum()                                <= .95]

        return bank_unmatched, je_unmatched


bank_rec, je_rec = recon()                    # Run function
```

Case 5

The Internal Revenue Service (IRS) is time bound on when it can challenge tax returns or collect back-taxes. Under current law, the IRS has 3 years from the filing date or due date of the tax return, whichever is later. In case of a *substantial understatement*, defined as greater than 25% of gross income, the IRS has up to 6 years. No time limit applies if the taxpayer fails to file a return, or if the IRS can establish fraud or a willful attempt to evade tax. These time limits are collectively known as the Statute of Limitations.

The IRS is performing a reverse examination of submitted returns. In an Excel file, it has noted down the return's unique ID, due date, filing date, reporting gross income, potential understatement, and if fraud is suspected. Columns are named as follows: ID, Due Date, Filing Date, Reported Income, Understatement, Suspected Fraud. The Suspected Fraud field is binary with possible values of "Y" or "N." The agency wants to use Python to calculate the end date of the statute of limitations for each return under audit. Dates are stored as text in mm/dd/yyyy format.

```
import pandas as pd
from datetime import datetime, timedelta
from dateutil.relativedelta import relativedelta    # Google this function

ret_data =
pd.read_excel(r"C:\Users\uname\Desktop\return_details.xlsx")

stat_list = []
end_date_list = []
```

```
for key, dd, fd, inc, us, fr in ret_data.itertuples(index = False, name =
None):
        dd = datetime.strptime(dd, "%m/%d/%Y")
        fd = datetime.strptime(fd, "%m/%d/%Y")

        if fr = "Y":
                stat_yr = "None"
                end_date = "None"

        elif us/(us + inc) > .25:
                stat_yr = 6
                end_date = datetime.strftime(max(dd, fd) +
                                relativedelta(years = 6), "%m/%d/%Y")

        else:
                stat_yr = 3
                end_date = datetime.strftime(max(dd, fd) +
                                relativedelta(years = 3), "%m/%d/%Y")

        stat_list.append(stat_yr)
        end_date_list.append(end_date)

ret_data["Statute Years"] = stat_list
ret_data["End Date"] = end_date_list

ret_data.to_excel(r"C:\Users\uname\Desktop\return_details_updated.
xl        sx", index = False)
```

CONCLUSION

Since its inception in 1991, Python has been embraced by professionals across various industries worldwide to develop robust solutions. Global technological and economic advancements have changed the way accountants and business professionals must approach modern challenges. They must adapt by learning new skills and rethinking their role for today and tomorrow.

As a general-purpose, business-friendly programming language, Python is currently being widely used in various fields. The industry establishment has already adopted its use. However, while there is vast literature on the integration of Python to achieve automation goals in design, web development, search engine optimization, game development, and other fields, little work has been produced for the benefit of accountants and other business professionals.

As a CPA with experience in data analytics and accounting, I have written this book using my experience with Python. I have employed this dynamic language to develop tools to improve my work, resolve challenges I faced, and design new ways to advance my productivity further and redefine my CPA role.

In this volume, I provide knowledge on the foundational concepts of Python along with the beginner libraries I feel are necessary for business work. I also include case studies to demonstrate real-life application of Python in tackling business and accounting problems. You should be decently familiar with the basics of Python and ready to learn advanced programming at this point. In volume 2, I go over advanced libraries in Python, which can help you read, modify, and write PDF files; build robots to automatically perform work; deploy OCR tools to extract text out of images; create, edit, and format Excel files and develop macros without VBA; and perform financial analysis and present value calculations.

Many accounting firms, including all the Big 4, are already using the latest and state-of-the-art technologies. The AICPA has rushed to overhaul the CPA exam to heavily include data analysis and new technologies. Changes in the curriculum are expected in early 2024. One can perhaps presume that there is a skills gap between what universities are currently teaching and what firms are expecting. Business professionals should view new technologies and AI/ML as an inevitability and prepare themselves to keep pace with their professions.

REFERENCES

1. Swetz FJ. Mathematical treasure: Mesopotamian accounting tokens. Mathematical Treasure: Mesopotamian Accounting Tokens | Mathematical Association of America. https://www.maa.org/press/periodicals/convergence/mathematical-treasure-mesopotamian-accounting-tokens. Published September 2012.
2. Evolution of Accounting and Accounting Terminology | Investopedia. https://www.investopedia.com/articles/08/accounting-history.asp. Published May 2021.
3. Gonzales-Lara JY. The history of accounting in the United States | San Ignacio University, Miami, Florida. https://www.academia.edu/40010642/The_history_of_accounting_in_the_United_States_The_history_of_accounting_in_the_United_States_Content
4. ldroyd D & Dobie A. Themes in the history of bookkeeping | The Routledge Companion to Accounting History, London. Published July 2008. ISBN 978-0-415-41094-6, Chapter 5, p. 96
5. Oldroyd D. The role of accounting in public expenditure and monetary policy in the first century ad roman empire | The Accounting Historians Journal, 22(2), 117–129. Published 1995. http://www.jstor.org/stable/40698165
6. Westland JC. Audit Analytics: Data Science for the Accounting Profession | Cham: Springer International Publishing. Published 2020. https://www.springer.com/gp/book/9783030490904
7. Fischer MJ. Luca Pacioli on Business Profits | Journal of Business Ethics, 25(4), 299–312. Published 2000. http://www.jstor.org/stable/25074319
8. Double Entry | Corporate Finance Institute. https://corporatefinanceinstitute.com/resources/knowledge/accounting/double-entry/
9. Carruthers BG & Espeland WN. Accounting for Rationality: Double-Entry Bookkeeping and the Rhetoric of Economic Rationality | American Journal of Sociology, 97(1), 31–69. Published 1991. http://www.jstor.org/stable/2781637
10. Willekens M & Lauwers L. Five hundred years of bookkeeping: A portrait of Luca Pacioli | *Tijdschrift voor Economie en Management*, *XXXIX*(3), 289-304. Published 1994. https://research.tilburguniversity.edu/en/publications/five-hundred-years-of-bookkeeping-a-portrait-of-luca-pacioli
11. Boyns T, Edwards J & Nikitin M. Accounting and the Industrial Revolution: A Comparison between Great Britain and France | Accounting Auditing Control, 2, 5-20. Published 1996. https://doi.org/10.3917/cca.021.0005
12. How humans invented this thing called accounting (a brief history) | ACCA Global. https://yourfuture.accaglobal.com/global/en/blog/how-humans-invented-accounting.html
13. Certified Public Accountant: How to Become a CPA? | Study. https://study.com/articles/Certified_Public_Accountant_How_to_Become_a_CPA.html
14. William Burroughs Adding Machine | Lemelson-MIT. https://lemelson.mit.edu/resources/william-burroughs
15. Cong Y, Du H & Vasarhelyi AM. Technological Disruption in Accounting and Auditing | Journal of Emerging Technologies in Accounting. Published September 2018; 15 (2): 1–10. https://doi.org/10.2308/jeta-10640

16. Yoon S. A Study on the Transformation of Accounting Based on New Technologies: Evidence from Korea. Sustainability. Published 2020; 12(20):8669. https://doi.org/10.3390/su12208669
17. How COVID-19 changed technology in accounting (and what the future looks like) | Karbon. https://karbonhq.com/resources/the-future-of-technology-in-accounting/
18. https://www.seagate.com/files/www-content/our-story/trends/files/idc-seagate-dataage-whitepaper.pdf
19. https://www.analyticsinsight.net/history-and-development-of-python-programming-language/
20. https://www.makeuseof.com/python-object-oriented-programming/
21. https://opensource.com/article/19/10/python-programming-paradigms
22. https://vilmate.com/blog/python-vs-other-programming-languages/
23. https://www.monocubed.com/advantages-of-python/
24. https://www.pyimagesearch.com/2017/07/10/using-tesseract-ocr-python/
25. https://stripe.com/docs/api/pagination
26. https://www.scribd.com/document/379538935/Employee-Payroll-System-Python
27. https://www.researchgate.net/publication/343558578_Market_Basket_Analysis_Recommendation_System_Using_Association_Rules
28. https://www.rapyd.net/blog/the-case-for-a-python-ecommerce-website/
29. https://www.geospatialworld.net/blogs/why-is-python-a-perfect-choice-for-big-data/
30. https://pythoninoffice.com/cashflow-projection-in-python/
31. https://www.ey.com/en_gl/assurance/how-can-artificial-intelligence-enhance-your-lease-accounting-approach
32. https://brainstation.io/career-guides/how-long-does-it-take-to-learn-python
33. https://blog.spendesk.com/en/accounting-automation
34. https://futurefirm.co/accounting-automation/
35. https://www.britannica.com/technology/automation/Advantages-and-disadvantages-of-automation
36. https://www.oreilly.com/radar/automated-coding-and-the-future-of-programming/
37. https://www.journalofaccountancy.com/newsletters/2020/feb/automated-machine-learning-tools.html
38. https://www.ssi-schaefer.com/en-th/best-practices-trends/trends/is-automation-only-for-large-companies-815866
39. https://thepythonguru.com/reasons-to-use-python-over-other-programming-languages/
40. https://www.millennium-project.org/challenge-3/
41. https://www.albawaba.com/business/global-economic-power-shift-g7-e7-states-2030-1326061
42. https://www.topuniversities.com/courses/computer-science-information-systems/5-trends-computer-science-research
43. https://www.toptal.com/finance/financial-modeling/python-and-finance
44. https://www.lighthouselabs.ca/en/blog/how-python-is-used-in-automation https://www.codemotion.com/magazine/Glossary/python-programming-language/

45. https://www.ifac.org/about-ifac/professional-accountants-business/news-events/2013-10/roles-and-importance-professional-accountants-business
46. https://www.cpaselfstudy.com/2020/04/17/the-aicpa-code-of-professional-conduct-what-you-need-to-know/
47. https://www.ifac.org/system/files/publications/files/ifac-code-of-ethics-for.pdf
48. https://www.journalofaccountancy.com/issues/2021/aug/how-cpas-helped-save-businesses-during-coronavirus-pandemic.html
49. https://www.ethicsboard.org/system/files/meetings/files/4864.pdf
50. https://us.aicpa.org/interestareas/accountingeducation/newsandpublications/should-accounting-students-code
51. https://www.tx.cpa/resources/txcpa-magazine/issue-details/septoct2021/2021/09/13/cpa-evolution-initiative-is-bringing-an-all-new-approach-to-cpa-licensing
52. https://www.tx.cpa/resources/txcpa-magazine/issue-details/septoct2021/2021/09/13/cpa-evolution-initiative-is-bringing-an-all-new-approach-to-cpa-licensing#:~:text=The%20CPA%20Evolution%20initiative%20is%20a%20joint%20project%20of%20the,future%2Dproofing%20the%20CPA%20profession.
53. https://wall.alphacoders.com/by_category.php?id=29&name=TV+Show+Wallpapers
54. https://www.aicpa.org/news/article/cpa-evolution-what-is-the-early-thinking-on-three-cpa-exam-disciplines
55. https://www.journalofaccountancy.com/news/2019/dec/new-cpa-licensure-model-201922573.html
56. https://www.xlwings.org/blog/reporting-with-python
57. https://www.stxnext.com/what-is-python-used-for/
58. https://www.investopedia.com/terms/v/visual-basic-for-applications-vba.asp
59. https://www.pwc.com/us/en/faculty-resource/assets/pwc-data-driven-paper-feb2015.pdf
60. https://fincad.com/blog/how-python-makes-data-science-more-accessible
61. https://www2.deloitte.com/us/en/insights/focus/cognitive-technologies/state-of-ai-and-intelligent-automation-in-business-survey.html
62. https://www.flexi.com/wp-content/uploads/2021/02/Flexi-Whitepaper-How-Accounting-and-Finance-are-Being-Transformed-by-AI.pdf
63. https://blog.paypie.com/cash-flow/small-business-cash-flow-statistics-the-list-to-end-all-lists/
64. https://www.forbes.com/2010/06/02/internet-software-zeus-technology-cloud-computing-10-garrett.html#5ce899c1424b
65. https://www.forbes.com/sites/theyec/20/09/10/ais-impact-on-accounting-and-finance/#707ba82fe855
66. https://www.vansystems.com/wp-content/uploads/2017/03/AP_shocking_stats.pdf
67. https://www.accountingtoday.com/news/accounting-software-market-to-reach-118b-by-2026
68. https://www.businesswire.com/news/home/20180918005146/en/MapR-and-Deloitte-Announce-Strategic-Alliance-to-Modernize-Analytics-and-Speed-AI-Success
69. https://acfeinsights.squarespace.com/acfe-insights/2018/12/14/how-artificial-intelligence-uncovered-evidence-of-fraud

70. https://aibusiness.com/document.asp?doc_id=760260
71. https://www.emailaudience.com/research-picture-worth-1000-words-marketing/
72. https://www.amanet.org/articles/using-visual-language-to-create-the-case-for-change/
73. https://datascienceparichay.com/article/understanding-joins-in-pandas

Made in the USA
Las Vegas, NV
03 November 2026

57424362R00096